THAT WHY CHILD

THAT WHY CHILD

Problems in Psychotherapy and Counselling

CAROL JEFFREY

Foreword by Dr Michael Fordham
With a Commentary on the Author's Paintings
from C. G. Jung

FREE ASSOCIATION BOOKS/LONDON/NEW YORK

Published in 1996 by
Free Association Books Ltd
57 Warren Street
London W1P 5PA
and 70 Washington Square South
New York, NY 10012–1091

ISBN 1 85343 338 1 hbk

A CIP catalogue record for this book is available
from the British Library.

Produced for Free Association Books Ltd by
Chase Production Services, Chipping Norton, OX7 5QR
Typeset by Stanford DTP Services, Milton Keynes
Printed in the EC by T.J. Press, Padstow

CONTENTS

LIST OF PLATES

Plates 1–13 between pages 80 and 81
and Plates 14–22 between pages 111 and 112.

The book is dedicated with my deepest love and gratitude, first, to the memory of my late husband Tom, who, from his generous nature, encouraged and supported me in everything I wanted to do or be, throughout the sixty abiding years of our relationship.

Also to my three children, Michael, Robin and Sally, who, with consistent loyalty and the eagerness of related independence, have taught me the basics of all I came to know about the developing individualities of children. Very special thanks again to my daughter Sally for so much patience in the arduous work of continual typing and retyping and valuable perceptive advice in the final task of editing. My thanks also to Elizabeth Best for her invaluable help in many practical matters.

I owe a debt of gratitude to The Open Way for essential support in the preparation of the pictures. So many friends, colleagues, patients and students have contributed to the experiences which form the book, that they cannot be thanked individually. So let all be thanked and honoured here.

PREFACE

Once, when she was about twenty-one, Carol Jeffrey was described as 'the sort of thing you would see looking at you from among the roots of a tree'. She calls herself a Celtic changeling, born on Halloween in 1898 from a Welsh father and an Irish mother. The staff at her school, however, spoke of her secretly among themselves as 'That Why Child'. (See Radio 4 and World Service Broadcasts July 1992 and 1993.)

The search for the 'Why and What for' of experience has always inspired her active interest and formed the permanent style of her work as a psychotherapist.

Educated at home by her mother (mornings only) until she was fifteen and never going to school, hers was certainly an unusual and somewhat idyllic childhood. 'There was freedom to roam the woods and fields, live in trees, play in the brooks, tend animals, help on the little farm. Then, for me there was sitting in the corn bin in the back kitchen reading history or literature to my mother while she did the washing, dressed a chicken or made jam. We would break off sometimes to sing or play music'.

'Such a girl will never catch up', the reluctant headmistress said when at last she entered school at fifteen. Frustrated by poverty in her first ambition to become a doctor, the next choice was teacher training. She did 'catch up', qualifying with the Post-Graduate Teaching Diploma.

Music filled a large part of her life. Piano began at five, small organ at seven, violin at ten, with singing as her chief musical talent. She became the organist of the little village church when she was twelve.

In 1925 after five years teaching Music and English, she married, and her teaching career was automatically ended by the most ignorant and short-sighted rule education ever made.

This did not stop the search for the Why of things, so she started
a little 'school' in her own home and among her own children. Three
or four children were chosen who had special needs, either in
learning or more often in emotional development, so that the
'school' became almost a mini child guidance clinic. This, together
with being on an Adult Education panel of lecturers in Child
Development, led to her taking the London University Post-
Graduate Diploma in Individual Psychology in 1944/5. She was then
immediately involved in the establishing of the new Child Guidance
Service in three districts in Kent.

Intensive work and experience in therapy developed in these
clinics and after two years she entered a long Jungian analysis with
Dr Michael Fordham. She describes this experience as 'an epic
encounter which expanded my knowledge and enhanced my
experience to a degree of fertile contentment which has remained
undiminished ever since.'

In 1952 Dr Graham Howe made her a founder member of The
Open Way Association, and a staff member of its Psychotherapy
Clinic. Full-time therapy in the Clinic led to the development of an
expanding private practice which has continued ever since. She also
had a large share in the psychological research work of the Open
Way Association. She was Secretary for a considerable time, and is
now Co-President with Dr Tom Farewell. The book records some of
the experiences of those fifty years.

Study of the massive works of Jung has been a vital and lasting
influence in the life-work of The Why Child and is, she says,
continuing to guide and inspire the process even now, in her 98th
year.

Together with this, the freedom and closeness to Nature of a
childhood in remote, almost primitive country would seem to have
ensured the inevitability for a life's work of enabling people to
become what by nature they truly are.

'It gives people to themselves.'

FOREWORD

Psychotherapy is a peculiar occupation. It does not appear to be a science like physics and chemistry, or even biology, because there is greater uncertainty about what is being done.

In the early days both Freud, Jung and some others were at pains to define their spheres of action, and in both, emphasis was laid on techniques, as if one could learn to be a psychotherapist by learning and applying some method. It was thought that in this way there could develop a standard procedure. To some extent that happened, so that an idea could be gained about how a psychoanalyst or an analytical psychologist would behave and what each school aimed to achieve.

It was soon found, however, that a personal factor entered into the relationship between analyst and patient. Furthermore, such a relationship led to so much uncertainty that many psychotherapists found it necessary to investigate with more care what they did, especially when their method proved unsuccessful. A change came about and experience often replaced theory and method, while imagination or literary skills could be more useful than scientific ones.

Carol Jeffrey is one of those who have the gift of expressing how they think and feel, and how their patients respond. We can find various models and psychological concepts often showing Jung's predominating influence, and this makes sufficient framework in which she sets her exposition. However, one never feels that the model is so used that her patient is an illustration of it. On the contrary, it is the model itself which becomes appropriate and even seems to grow out of her developing encounters with the patient. In this way she never departs far from experience, real or intuitive, whether it be her own or that of others.

There is nothing 'ordinary' about Carol Jeffrey, nor her remarkable children either, and one is frequently left startled or lost in

xiii

admiration for her sensitiveness and skill with her patients, her
children and herself.

Being a psychotherapist requires constant attention to one's own
inner world which develops and is fertilized by the therapist's relationships – especially with his or her patients. The psychotherapist
thus stands halfway between being a scientist and being an artist. It
may seem as if Carol Jeffrey's work is an art, but it contains data which
are also objective and so scientific. It is a thought-provoking book
and one which will be read by psychotherapists, but the ordinary
enquiring reader will also gain a rich experience of how a gifted
psychotherapist works, for this book depicts the process honestly
and with a minimum of presuppositions and technical terminology.

Michael Fordham
1994

INTRODUCTION

This book is about problems. If you had a problem around 1898 in the village where I was born, you had two choices. First, if it was life-threatening and castor-oil and mustard plaster had done no good, then a horse would be found to take a relative or a neighbour to fetch the nearest doctor from seven miles away. Second, if the problem was 'in your head', and bad enough to be life-threatening to other people, and neither help from the church, nor the full-moon midnight ceremony at the crossroads had worked, then the horse would cart you off the fifteen miles to the nearest lunatic asylum.

Nowadays, almost 100 years later, things are very different. Problem solving, particularly 'in the head' has become a vast science parallel with physical Medicine. In addition, a whole varied range of centres, training courses, foundations and individual exponents of 'alternatives' have developed to contribute to the huge expansion of the medically based established societies. Unlike Medicine, however, psychological research often makes use also of integrates and insights from such sources as Religion, Philosophy and Mythology.

THE THERAPEUTAE

'The Therapeutae' was a religious group of 'healers' in the first century AD. The word 'therapy' meant 'waiting upon', and a therapist was a servant. I have always liked the idea of a psychotherapist 'waiting', and the book contains vignettes from fifty years' experience as a psychotherapist, where often the waiting game was a crucial feature.

THE PROBLEM OF FEAR

Standing beside, attentively waiting, I have found particularly rewarding if the problem is Fear; especially with a child. A child's

1

fear is monstrous and life-threatening to his immature resources. He
hides, desperate, under an ever-thickening lid which often is his
only shelter. We must never force an entry, but wait, with beneficent
stillness until the lid lifts of itself and we may be invited in. Many
times I have found that this kind of prolonged patient waiting has
proved to be the key to recovery from an autistic state, after every
other approach had failed. (See Chapter 2, 'Silent Children'.) With
adults, remotely hidden fear is very often revealed to be at the
bottom of various problematic states of mind, where at first neither
the patient nor the therapist suspects it. Here, 'waiting' may need
to be unbelievably extended, while theory stands aside. (See
Chapter 4, 'Fear and Anxiety'.)

DEPRESSION

By contrast, in cases of depression (see Chapter 5, 'Studies in
Depression'), open therapy may not always need much waiting time.
Lethargy and paralysis are likely to express the problem and the
method may sometimes be more active and immediate.

COUNSELLING

I have included counselling because that newer discipline will have
much in common with psychotherapy as it moves towards professional status. It seems to me that the differences in such things as
depth, length of commitment, training and experience, do not
prevent both disciplines from sharing the same basic principles of
motive and method.

INFLUENCE OF C.G. JUNG

I did not meet Jung in the flesh, but his influence on my development as a therapist, and in my life generally, has been widespread.
The stimulation of his thinking and his unique penetration into the
meaning and mystery of human life came from study of his massive
writings. But the dynamic contact I had with the man himself came
first from a few letters he wrote to me, which included his deep interpretation of my drawings, (see Chapter 11, 'The Peacock's Lifecycle').
Of great importance also were the numerous vivid and challenging
dreams about him which I experienced during the twelve years or
so before his death.

In the dreams, Jung would appear, sometimes as a voice, in answer to an appeal, or in person at crisis moments in my work or my life, giving me advice, answering queries or probing deep into unrecognized areas of my psyche. Twice, to my astonishment, he referred in a dream to the nearness and preparation for his own death. While I was dreaming so much about Jung, I did not at first realize that the use of dreams was so central in his practice. Perhaps unconsciously I did 'know', because I have always found working with a patient's dreams to be the most powerful and productive relation between us. (See Chapter 10, 'Dreams'.)

THE OPEN WAY CHARITABLE TRUST. 'WITHOUT THE RULES'.

In the early days it was very difficult to combine my new and untried method with the demands of the established orthodoxy, and in this Jung's inward influence was crucial, especially at first when an independent position was painful and precarious.

At this time Dr Graham Howe was the first effective rescuing influence I encountered in those desperate confused days immediately after the last war. I was pioneering in a sticky network which developed in the severe teething troubles of the new Child Guidance Service. We started in the last year of the war when trained and experienced staff were in very short supply – or even non-existent. One psychiatrist and I set up three clinics serving quite a wide area. To begin with, the two of us shared all the roles. We divided the psychotherapy equally between us, the psychiatrist took on psychiatric and secretarial work. I doubled as Educational Psychologist and Psychiatric Social worker (PSW). Later on, one clinic acquired a PSW and Secretary. In this way, I encountered hastily constructed rules and limitations which threatened my work and involvement in helping to bring to birth the new Child Guidance Service. The boundaries within which I had to work, seemed militarized and as jealously guarded as the Berlin Wall. Graham Howe had the status and the authority to brush aside narrow limits and regulations, even if it broke the rules – and it often did! He did not care much for rules, and was always ready to encourage independent foresight in thought and action.

After the war, Graham Howe became disillusioned with the slow and sometimes confused progress of the psychotherapeutic scene in general. So with great energy he collected a quickly growing group of like-minded searching people and set us to work to make more open methods of therapy and its exponents much more freely available.

He founded The Open Way Clinic of Psychotherapy in London in 1953, and by involving me permanently in its founding and functioning, he provided liberal and sheltered opportunity within which I had freedom to work from a basis of individual real experience.

A little later I worked in close collaboration with Dr Alfred Torrie and Dr R.D. Laing, who were both directors of the Clinic for a number of years. From this I had the outward confirmation and from Jung's philosophy the inward permission to trust intuitive and visionary insight. An awesome confidence arises when I can put theory aside and wait – alert and welcoming – for those magnificent moments when some unique individual emergence is taking place in the psyche of a patient, creating its own theory as the mind arranges experience.

Jung's close colleague Dr Henry Baynes (1949) wrote, 'The human psyche cannot be charted with callipers, and all those ingenious mechanisms, so cunningly contrived to exclude the human variable, only succeed perfectly in excluding the soul.' My passionate belief in the priority of the human variable has governed my choice of a more independent and individually based method. At the same time, I do recognize, emphatically, that techniques of therapy, structure and models have been painstakingly researched and constructed over a long time by many fine and dedicated minds. The great responsibilities of the medical profession have governed and nurtured the development of organized method, structures and boundaries, thus giving reliability and discipline to the newly emerging profession. Outstanding among the analysts has been Dr Michael Fordham, one of Jung's close colleagues and co-editor of *Jung's Collected Works*. Dr Fordham is always to be found in the vanguard of development, and he has done major work to establish and maintain a healthy and productive balance between the boundaries of theoretical structure and independent freedom in the therapeutic discipline.

There have been many occasions in my practice when I have witnessed in the psyche of a patient the emergence of a highly individual and valuable insight, or an inspired solution to a problem in his life or mind which was as yet unrecognized or unsolved within the same area in my own psyche. Then I say, 'We must now change chairs.' Sometimes we do in reality, and the symbolic gesture has been richly rewarding and productive for both of us. It is at such moments that I seem to see the callipers and the human variable come together in a creative and harmonious partnership as vividly illustrated in this challenging dream of mine about Jung.

SEARCH OF A TRAIN

In the dream, I was in a special train, which had been organized entirely to take professional delegates to an important International conference on Jungian Psychology, somewhere in Europe. Every carriage was full of eminent-looking analysts and leading authorities in the profession. All I saw were men, dressed immaculately in most elegant clothes. I was walking along the corridor looking in through each glass door at carriages full of these superior-looking delegates, and as I searched the train from end to end, without finding a seat, I became increasingly anxious and insecure about my own status and acceptance in such a formidable group. The question of dress suggested further humiliation as I was wearing very ordinary clothes, and boots I wear for gardening. There seemed no place for me, as I neared the end of this *double first class* train. At the last carriage, I opened a door in the corridor and entered a rough and ready luggage van, a bit dark and dusty, and full of boxes and crates, creaking and chattering among themselves, almost as if they were alive and enjoying the rough jostling of the journey. Then, in the half-light I saw Jung, perched on an old wooden crate, smoking a pipe and dressed in TREE BARK! It was an ordinary suit, but made entirely of brown ridged tree bark. Strangely – or perhaps not? – it did not strike me as odd; I think I said to myself, 'Oh yes, of course.' Jung smiled and said 'Ah, you've found me then.' And he made room for me to sit beside him on the old crate.

The challenge for me in this dream was that I should search to develop in myself relationship and shared functioning between this particular pair of opposites. The *first class carriage people* with their structures and theories within my own personality needed to become colleagues – instead of opponents – with the *freedom-loving garden and earthy kind of people* in the luggage van area of my psyche. Jung himself counted this reconciliation among the fundamentals of his life work. A challenge for me indeed, and now, at ninety-seven, one in which I am still engaged.

ANALYSIS

My analysis with Dr Michael Fordham was an inner life experience whose deeper influence it would be difficult to overvalue. The work with him spread over twenty years, and because the profound chrism of such an epic encounter cannot easily be put into words, I can say here only that the meeting and journeying of our two personalities expanded and enhanced my experience to a degree of fertile contentment which has remained undiminished ever since.

Concerned with the motivations and goals of such a mutual enterprise, lasting for so many years, there are inevitably struggles, battles, successes and failures; there is hope and despair, famine and sudden plenty. We experienced in ourselves – and reflected also in each other – brilliant insights and blind misunderstanding, conflict and co-operation, separateness and relating, and all those swings of opposites whose teleology pulls forward all development.

It is a very special pleasure to me that Michael Fordham consented to write the Foreword to my book.

1

HEROIC ADAPTATION

HOW CAN I NOT BE WRONG?

KATIE, HANNAH AND FREDA

These three people all presented a problem of deep and almost total dissatisfaction with themselves, and chronic delay and inhibition in basic impulse patterns. The two adult women could not understand why this should be so. They were highly competent people with successful jobs, good marriages and healthy, independent children. They both said they were obsessed by anxiety that whatever they did, 'it might not be right', and likely to cause harm or disaster. No outside reason for this had ever been found, although sincere work on the problem had been carried out. 'Je m'accuse de tout ce que je vais faire.'

The breakthrough for me in knowing what to do came when one woman was repeating again and again – 'I am always afraid that whatever I intend to do may not be the right choice.' I replied 'It is worse than that! You are certain that whatever you do will be wrong. You have no choice!' The flood of relief which surged up in her was dramatic. She said over and over again, 'Yes, yes, that's it! How *can* I not be wrong? Everything I do will be wrong.' This indicated to me just when this barrier had been set up. It must have been very early in infancy. A young baby has very little choice of action. In her case it seemed to me that very early in her life, all choice had been denied her.

We approached this problem with the open system where all my own thoughts and theoretical ideas were deliberately screened off. This was something I learned to do when I was taking IQ tests with children. I found that the validity of a test could be disrupted if I allowed the form of the answer in my own mind to be transferred to the subconscious area of the child's mind, where 'knowledge' of the answer had not yet organized itself into a verbally expressed idea. Several times I noticed that when a child was unable to give an answer, if I said, 'You are going to be right', the correct reply would come at once. Often I would deliberately think of some

7

irrelevant event or memory, and turn my body away from the child. By encouraging this woman to re-experience her dreams emotionally and physically, she came to be able to create her own diagnosis and place it correctly at the precise point where it began in her life. (See Chapter 10, 'Dreams'.) It was similar with the other woman, where the blockage was located early in her second year.

The little girl, Katie, had made a conscious choice of her style of action, but she shared with the two women the same heroic adaptation, in that each one had steadfastly contained the complex within her own psyche. By bearing alone this responsibility, they had prevented the problematic burden from being projected on to anyone else, including their own children. Because of the very positive and exclusive nature of such a chosen style of life, growing from so early a point, the task of therapy to develop a balance was long and very gradual. Here again, the new concept had to be created as 'gut-knowledge', equally – if not more so – than in the mental sphere of intellect and conscious thought.

Katie

Born an orphan, Katie had been moved from one *home* to another eight times before her ninth birthday. The last move was to a foster mother who brought her to me complaining that she could not cope with such a strange child.

> 'She's as good as gold – always has been, they say, but she gives me the creeps with her silent, old-fashioned ways. She's always reading and she doesn't talk or play like a child at all. I'm sure she's unhappy but I can't get through to her any way. I'm no good to her and I would like her to go somewhere else.'

At first, Katie seemed exactly like that report, except that she didn't *give me the creeps*! She was very interesting to me, for it was like being with an intensely introverted adult. It was true that she did not act or play spontaneously, and our activities and games were initiated and maintained mostly by me. Unless asked to speak, she remained silent, and most of my questions were rhetorical so as not to invade her introversion.

After some weeks of my usual 'waiting time', I felt a development in her relation to me. I said I had to write a letter and would she use the sand tray by herself for a few minutes? She complied as usual and I went across the room to write at my table. I wrote, and Katie stood still as a statue at the sand tray, not building or using any figures. Her only movement was to trickle sand through the fingers of one hand. I continued 'writing' and silence and stillness reigned for about twenty minutes. Then suddenly the little statue spoke:

'You can never do what you want to do can you?'
I said – 'Oh, can't you? I wonder why that is?'
'Because you always have to do your duty.'
'Well yes, I suppose you have to do your duty. But then ... what you *want* to do ... do you think they might sometimes be the same?'

Katie shook her head slightly and the sand trickling began again. I continued 'writing'. Suddenly, she dusted the sand from her hand and came over to me. Putting her hands on my knees, she gazed up at me with a heavy intensity and slowly asked:

'Are they the same for you?'
'Well yes, I think quite often those things are the same for me.'

Her next question was rapped out with the speed of an investigating lawyer at a trial:

'Are you doing it now?'

Fortunately I could answer truthfully.

'Yes, I am doing it now, because this is my job, my duty, but I do also want to be here with you.'

Katie smiled slightly and returned to the sand. The difference now was that she used both hands and made a little mountain in the sand with a cave in the side, and added a couple of trees to the scene.
All at once she looked across at me and in a loud accusing voice asked:

'Do they *pay* you for doing this?'
'Yes, they pay me, because this is my job, so I get paid.'

Again a nod and a tiny smile and the silent sand play continued. After six or seven minutes, she suddenly dusted off her hands, strode across the room to me, and, hands on my knees and large dark eyes searching like a judge, she put me to the final test.

'Would you give this job up for all the money in the world?'

There could be only one answer and at that moment I felt it to be
true. What was confronting me was much more than a nine-year-
old little girl.

'No Katie, I would *not* give this job up for all the money in the world.'

Katie came to life at once and with a new vigour and passion in her
voice she said:

'Then I shall tell you what I am going to do when I am grown up. I am
going to nurse lepers, because lepers are poor ill people and they have a
horrible disease and are all ugly and funny shapes, and nobody will go near
them and they have to live in caves all alone, so I am going to nurse them.'

I searched until I found a children's home where the matron burst
into tears when I told her this story. I took Katie there and visited
her after six months to find her completely happy and competently
looking after a group of toddlers.

'She's one of our best nurses, the babies adore her.'

So, for Katie, the gap had narrowed with duty and natural impulse
coming together.

Hannah

When I met Hannah, she was nearly forty, a very well related wife
and mother. Her life-long career has been outstandingly successful
and contributory, as well as rewarding to herself. Surprisingly,
however, the happiness and confidence you would expect have been
denied her. Always, her consciousness has been overshadowed by
the unrelenting thought: 'How *can* I not be wrong'?
    Her physical body has often been invaded by the same mysterious
imperative. In spite of this, Hannah has steadfastly contained the
complex within herself, and has totally prevented its influence from
falling on her own children or others. I judge such a lifestyle as
'heroic'.
    Hannah's parents and family were involved in medicine and
education in another country. They – especially her mother – were

very ambitious for their first child to enter a high-ranking career of international fame. So, at the age of two, as well as lessons at home with mother, Hannah was sent to a day school where work and not play was the daily routine. Each child started the day with 100 marks, and a mark was deducted for every mistake or lapse of standard in work or behaviour.

Imagine a two-year-old child being able to go home at the end of the day with 100 per cent! But Hannah's mother's terrifying anxiety demanded it, and she was punished if she had 99 per cent or less. The same 100 per cent was demanded at home as well, and fingers were rapped to indicate mistakes.

There was more in Hannah's childhood experience which added to the doubt and despair of ever being 100 per cent in all activity. Could she ever 'not be wrong?'

Freda

Freda at fifty was depressed and chronically anxious, severely over-controlled and often obsequious in behaviour with other people. She could not walk in front of anyone else, or go through a door unless she was last. Speaking was hesitant and often fragmented, although the content of what she said was always perceptive and well thought out. Whatever she writes is fluent and expressive, but chronic anxiety has forced her to monitor every spoken word and phrase. She felt that whatever proceeded out of her mouth must hesitate or change, and would be sure to be rejected or bring punishment or humiliation. Her typical word was 'sorry', which invaded her conversation. Even if someone else dropped something, Freda would instantly say 'Sorry!'

Just as with Hannah, Freda's life is also 'heroic' for she has a good marriage, three healthy, independent children and makes a very useful contribution to the community. Most of all, she has faithfully contained and suffered the problem within herself, consciously preventing the conflict from being projected on to anyone else.

Freda's problem began in the early sabotage of life's first impulse – that is to seek and obtain food – a baby's sole function between itself and the outside world.

Freda's mother had been trained by her own mother as follows:

'When you are breast-feeding your baby, whenever she grasps the nipple greedily, give her cheek a smart tap and make her wait before you allow her to suck. You must let her know as soon as possible who is boss!'

So the vital impulse was trained to hesitate, to delay and fear. This routine was strictly carried out in other aspects of discipline throughout the whole of Freda's childhood, especially at meal times; where, if any one of the many extreme rules was imperfectly obeyed, a long cane was always on the table to remind the offender. Feeding is the prototype of all survival functioning, expressing the baby's overwhelming need to maintain life itself. This is the baby's first and only choice, and the development of confidence, fulfilment and safety all have their origin in its satisfaction.

The sabotage of a confident development of this comprehensive function has spread over a wide range of Freda's life. Freda's own mother had been subjected to the same training and probably her mother also. These women were governed by intense anxiety which they did not understand at all – an anxiety built up in human experience ever since the birth of consciousness.

THE COLLECTIVE LEVEL

It is important that we should recognize this deep collective level of the fear which drove these mothers to behave in so extreme a way to their daughters. They were unable to mediate the power of the total Mother Archetype which overwhelmed them and their undefended children.

Hannah and Freda, however, as the therapeutic relationship developed, were able to recognize and balance both sides of the personality of their mothers. They both described the terrifying, 'almost god-like' punitive authority, but also, a protective natural mother who could introduce them eagerly to nature and music, and care for them tenderly if they were ill.

Katie, Hannah and Freda all presented a deep dimension. They are 'Carriers': an honourable category where a sensitive individual is loaded with heavy collective memories of human experience of all time. A complex constructed by 'training', as with Hannah and Freda, constitutes a very good screen or hook for these collective conflicts to project on to.

CARRIERS

I see increasing numbers of women who are burdened with such chronic loads to which they are unconsciously sensitive. These complexes, often of guilt and inferiority – have been built into humanity's psychosomatic record ever since the choice was made for a new function of consciousness to emerge from instinctive Paradise. Several women have told me that they have suffered life-long mysterious anxiety which forces them to placate, or to expiate. Consciously they cannot explain this at all. A very capable and well related mother and grandmother of splendid children said:

'However hard I try to work and to live a good life, I am all the time obsessed with the feeling that I must appease, pacify and placate – it never seems enough.'

Another woman whose spontaneous activity was almost paralysed by severe phobias for many normal physical actions as well as conduct generally, told me that she had a continual powerful conviction that she was a grossly inferior being. She felt that anything she might do, or even want to do, would be bad or dangerous. She said she thought it was 'to do with being a woman'.

ADRENAL GUILT

When a Carrier first begins to research into the origins of this kind of chronic guilt complex, the therapeutic journey is often long and difficult as we meet with heavy and terror-stricken barriers and resistance. Sometimes there is a sudden breakthrough when the realization comes that this is a collective problem and not exclusive or even belonging to an individual person. Then the function of the Carrier can develop more positively as this new knowledge begins to break the chain of ancestral unconscious conflict.

THE ADRENALIN ANALOGY

Adrenalin is the initiator of physical action in all animal life – the essential fuel of energy. It is called out before any impulse can go forward. We cannot lift a finger, run a mile, wield a sword, blink an eyelid or shed a tear without the bloodstream receiving it and

transporting it to appropriate organs. The secreting of this essential
hormone is an entirely spontaneous impulse whose function is not
interfered with in all other species. But the 'un-animal' part of
humanity has – alas – acquired the ability to delay, suppress and
forbid spontaneous impulse. The human body, especially the female
body, has constructed barriers and diversions to instinctive activity
which often confuse and change goals and motivation. It is the
recognition and assimilation of this dimension of 'knowledge' which
makes successful therapy possible.

PSYCHOTHERAPY – AND AFTER

Psychotherapy with Katie was quite short, and its gift to her lay in
the assurance I could give her in the fundamental value of her own
person. 'Worth more to me than all the money in the world'. Her
career was set to become the matron of a children's home, so she
only had to substitute orphan children for lepers.

Freda and Hannah gained a great deal from long-term therapy. In
one sense it has never ended with them, for they are both now fully
trained therapists themselves. Their work there is outstanding.

2

SILENT CHILDREN

A STUDY OF WITHDRAWAL IN AUTISTIC AND SCHIZOID CHILDREN

The Silent Children we shall be discussing in this chapter were referred to me privately or in Child Guidance Clinics. The referral reports varied from 'Depressed', 'Withdrawn' etc. to 'Schizoid' or 'Autistic' and in each case the child had become unable to speak, or never had talked much or at all. Progress was often slow and difficult, but if I was able to withhold any action and wait patiently enough until the child could make the first move, then the deep-seated problem would become open to treatment. A majority of these children had experienced other therapies which had failed, probably because this vital waiting time was impossible through pressures from *turnover* demands, lack of time and often anxiety of parents, therapists or authorities.

THE CHOICE OF A WAY OF LIFE

Neurosis and Psychosis are often revealed to have been *chosen* as a way of life – maybe the best or the only way an individual could tolerate the impact of an environment which was felt to be hostile, punitive and threateningly destructive. Some of the children I have seen have made several choices – one after another – as the symptoms of each choice were dissolved by methods which had, nevertheless, failed to reach the basic problem. Each new chosen system expressed the desperate effort to cope with and provide protection against what seemed to be impossible demands and a retaliatory climate. An example of this was Sylvia, who, by the time she was fifteen, had made three choices.

SYLVIA – EPILEPTIC? MENTAL DEFECTIVE? OR PLAIN DELINQUENT?

Sylvia, at fifteen, was said to be mentally deficient, unable to cope with school, speech distorted and largely incoherent. Physically she

15

was well-grown but uncoordinated in many movements. She could not use her arms and hands in normal ways, and if asked to lift or carry anything, she would say it hurt and would drop it. Her mother tried to involve her in simple housework, but to no avail. She hung her arms limply and said, 'I can't, it hurts.' Walking, however, was fairly normal. Having been asked if the girl could be brought to London to see me, I said, 'No, I will come to Reading and spend a day with you as a visitor.' I often did this kind of thing, and earned much disapproval from orthodox authorities! Anyhow, I found it usually paid very high dividends. So I spent a day with the family, and just observed what went on.

All was as the mother had told me, with one glaring exception – the girl could play the piano quite well, especially dance tunes, with good timing and accuracy. She had never had lessons but just copied by ear what she had heard on the radio, etc.; she didn't read music at all. This set me thinking deeply, though not really consciously, for I had no idea how I was going to treat the child. I offered to try, if she could be brought to London regularly, and we started. When she spoke, her phrases didn't make much sense quite often, or have much grammatical construction, and her drawing (which she did fairly readily) was crude and at about a four-year-old's level.

After several seemingly unfruitful sessions – we couldn't really hold a conversation – I suddenly suggested that she should lie down on the couch and go to sleep. She complied quite readily and I dreamily *talked* her into sleep, keeping my body very close to hers, just as you would with a baby. She seemed to sleep quite naturally for about fifteen minutes, and when she awoke she looked at me and my nearness, sat straight up and talked to me much more normally for about ten minutes. Then she seemed to tire, and relapsed into the habitual *defective* state. I asked her to try and draw what it felt like 'when things don't seem nice for you'. She drew in black and red, a large crude brick building engulfed in flames. She said it was 'a factory burning'. The 'normal' period ended here, so I had to wait until the next session to return to the drawing. After the sleep, I asked her to draw what was burning in the factory and now she produced a large, awkward-looking drawing of two enormous arms and hands, with chains and padlocks tying them up! I asked her if her arms felt like that – all chained and locked up and burning inside, and she shivered and cried and said, 'It's so hot, and it hurts all the time.'

Then the regression began, but I felt I knew how to proceed, and I visited the family again in Reading, and got a full account of Sylvia's childhood from her parents. I had not heard much of this before, and Sylvia had not been told at all.

Sylvia's Childhood

She was a very normal baby, but developed facial eczema at three months. A medical specialist (in London) ordered her arms to be enclosed in rigid splints from shoulder to wrist continuously, to prevent scratching! He said 'Don't remove the splints except for washing and then hold her hands. I don't want to see her again until the eczema is cured.' Can you believe that these splints stayed on continuously for the next *six months* of that baby's early development, so that when she was released at nine months, the imprisoned energies of the little creature's vital functions were suddenly freed, and she immediately plunged into *major epilepsy*, according to the doctors, and was treated for it with the usual drugs until she was nine. Because there was no improvement, her parents consulted a chiropractor who 'cured' the so-called epilepsy. She then immediately became *mentally deficient* which had not been suggested before – and the inability to use her arms became much worse. So it seemed to me that I was now expected to 'cure' the mental defect, and I wondered, if I did, what new symptom would take its place in the established pattern! Well, of course, I didn't try to 'cure' anything, but continued with the 'body work' of the sleeping state of physical safety and security, leading to the testing-out of normal reaction for a short time.

But these normal periods began to get longer and longer, and in them we were able to discuss, almost like adults, the trauma of her early months (which she had never been told before) and the understanding and re-experiencing of that gradually restored her abilities. What happened in these 'normal' periods (as they gradually increased to take up the whole hour), was that our discussions about the drawings and actual facts of the original trauma, enabled her to join up the entirely unconscious *body knowledge* with her fifteen-year-old judging function, in a conscious co-operation.

Happily I can tell you that within two years she had recovered well, and later trained as an assistant teacher in an Occupation Centre, where her piano playing came into its own. Music, and the piano, had been the one vital thing which could really flow in her arms and hands.

The kind of threat to life which such a child experiences – the menace of an environment or conditions which threaten to destroy – can come from outside the child, from people or climate or events, or from inside the personality when the pressure of powers and passionate energies are more than the child can express without retaliation from outside. These frustrated energies are then converted into symptoms like Sylvia's 'epilepsy'.

LUCY

Here is an example of the way in which a so-called *character disorder* in a little girl of two and a half was based on her very effective choice of a method to support her own survival. Her splendid choice was maintained for over two years, and the description in the referral report was 'a case of severe psychotic type, continual violent aggression, mutism and refusal to carry out any requests or instructions'. Lucy could hardly speak except to shout – usually 'No! No!', or scream some kind of abusive sound.

She was born with bad squints in both eyes, and at ten months was hospitalized, without her mother. Screaming with fright, she was anaesthetized and both eyes were operated on. Both eyes were then blindfolded with bandages. Her hands were tied to the side of the cot to prevent her from tearing off her bandages. When she awoke her world had disappeared. She had no eyes. New pain tore at the place where they had been. She could not move her arms or hands. Mother had disappeared. Strange hands and voices assaulted her in unfamiliar routines. What was she to do? As I said, she chose a splendid method – she *decided* to fight for her life.

Many times I had to remind her distracted parents that she was *fighting for her life*, when she was, in their words, 'being so naughty and violent'. Would they wish it otherwise! So in the hospital she screamed and heaved and kicked as she lay there, blind and tied to the cot, until the nursing staff were fed up and impotent to deal with 'such a difficult child'. She was surrounded by this threatening atmosphere for the whole of fourteen days, before the blindfold was removed and her hands were released. Her mother had not been allowed to visit her at all (it was not an English hospital and the more enlightened methods of child treatment had not reached it). So when her mother came to fetch her she had lost all faith in the *goodness* of everything and everybody. It is likely that her conscious memory of her mother would have failed also. It was inconceivable that she could turn into a 'good, trusting, loving little girl' again. Nothing could explain to her what had happened. She was only ten months old!

So with great strength and body wisdom, she stuck to her method of fighting for survival, and as this met with increasing rejection and restrictions from uncomprehending adults, they too – and especially her mother – became part of the untrustworthy, hostile and persecutory world around her. Her only protection was her own aggression against the Reality World which seemed out to destroy her.

To add to this, her own natural impulses – carried forward on the aggressive tide – also came under the retaliatory control efforts of the adults, and so the impact of her violent fighting was turned round upon herself, conditioning both the outer and inner climate in which she was living.

I saw this child privately in the nursing home where she was kept in a basement ward, as far away as possible from the nervous wreck of her mother in care on the top floor. The two had to be kept apart because immediately they met, Lucy attacked her mother, tearing at her face and eyes. I witnessed this almost psychotic attack when I asked the staff to bring them together, and I had to intervene quickly to prevent real injury to the mother as well as terror and confusion in the child.

What I did for Lucy was very risky and could have exacerbated the problem. However, trusting intuition more than reason, I sent her to a residential nursery school where a nurse was willing to carry out my experiment. What I intended was that to some extent the trauma of the hospital should be partly repeated; that is, she was 'sent away' to strange surroundings, *without her mother*. But this time, no hostile events followed. After four weeks, her mother came, and the nurse had learned what to do. Although she was prevented from attacking her mother, she was told she was a 'good girl' and plenty of play was safely organized – including Mother. There were several meetings in the day, and when Mother left, she promised to return in three weeks' time. This interval was repeated twice. I monitored these first meetings, until the nurse had learned the method. After the fourth meeting, Mother promised to come after two weeks, repeated twice and so on. Then at an interval of ten days (twice), then a week (twice), always with the promise to return at an exact time. Eventually, she came and went every day until trust had been established. Then for a week she stayed in the 'school' and at the end of that enough trust in Mother's coming had developed and the two were able to go home together and begin to build up a more normal relationship within the family setting. Lucy also began to talk normally as Reality became less threatening. We did it with a calendar of coloured ribbons which were detached daily until the *Mother coming* ribbon was reached. Lucy developed very well at home and at school.

I saw her again when she was twelve for a few sessions – to help her to understand in full consciousness why she was bothered every now and again by a sudden impulse to 'tear something to pieces!' She was a highly intelligent child and was intrigued and delighted to hear about our meeting ten years before. Lucy was a physically very strong child – as her attacks proved – and she was also mentally and emotionally robust. A weaker child might have simply given up and fallen into chronic depressive illness – or psychosis.

AUTISM AND THE SCHIZOPHRENIC FUNCTION

The state of withdrawal from reality which is called Autism in children has a majority of characteristics in common with Schizophrenia – which is more common in adults. The basis of both these disorders lies in the altered relationship with Reality where symptoms range from undue introversion, shyness and anxiety, through more severe states of withdrawal, unrelatedness to people, autism and finally to the extreme of catatonic schizophrenia. All the same, the boundaries between these multiple degrees are by no means definite and they merge and overlap, especially during treatment or when environmental changes take place.

There may be high intelligence – near genius sometimes – or mental retardation. Idiopathic autism is seen in children when the condition is primary, and successful treatment is unlikely. I had only one child referred whose autism seemed to be idiopathic, and I transferred him to a consultant who treated him for ten years without any sustained improvement.

HANDLING CHANGES IN BEHAVIOUR

Even when a child does *live in a world of his own*, (the common description of an autistic child), a contrast to this may be present – intermittently, rarely, or often. This is extremely important in the handling of withdrawn, depressed children (or adults), for these depressed, mute and compliant characters can change into the opposite type as they begin to get better. Then we are, or should be, delighted to witness rages, temper tantrums, panics, violence and all kinds of aggressive behaviour, as repressions are lifted and energies released.

An example of this was Sheila, aged ten, who began quite mute and stood paralysed in the middle of the floor when I first saw her. She stood like a puppet, with her limbs only moving if I moved them for her. I went along with this for many weeks, doing her movements for her, gradually increasing what we did to games – where I played both parts but involved her hands, for example and always referring to my/her moves as 'Sheila'.

The breakthrough for Sheila came first in her ability to move about the room and start to draw and play with objects, without my body doing it. She still did not speak, and I never asked her to. Then one day she gestured me to lie down on the couch. She then took a large, heavy window pole, jumped astride the couch, and threatening me with the pole, said loudly: 'Go to sleep!' I had to risk it – I had no choice. 'Shut your eyes,' was the next command, and with my eyes shut I listened to various movements as she flourished the stick and shook the couch. After a few minutes of this pretended sleep – I even tried to snore gently – everything went very quiet and still. She got down, fetched a cushion and blanket, covered me up and kissed my hair. After this she began to talk and later to play strenuous physical games with me, and sometimes she would let me chase her.

This kind of change is usually favourable, provided it can be properly handled. This will mean unusual tolerance on the part of parents, teachers, therapists and others who are important adults in the child's now changing world. When he is in this period of change-over, it is essential for him to be allowed to get the emotion out, to establish this flow, or perhaps torrent, and at the same time to learn how to integrate and organize the releasing energies into acceptable behaviour patterns. I once had a fifteen-year-old boy come at me with a jackknife, and there was no time for psychological reflection. My body reacted and I pressed myself right up against him and he dropped the knife and burst into tears. We could then talk as pals.

Both the boy and I were lucky that time. But only too often, especially in the early life of a child, this primary dynamic flow of energy and emotion is stopped, punished or repressed – either in its original movement, or, as with Sheila, in a release after repression. We are apt to restrict or forbid behaviour that expresses aggressive or sexual impulses in our children.

MARGARET

Margaret was six and in very poor health. She did not speak at all
and had never said more than a few isolated words or phrases which
she would scream while sleepwalking. The usual phrase was 'I want
it! I want it!' When awake she was completely mute, and appeared
to be paralysed by a terror. Her mother was a very large, noisy woman
who had five older boys, and she described Margaret as a 'poor little
runt'! She would bring the child to the clinic and literally push her
into the room – not unkindly, but with relative force because
Margaret was so thin and tiny. The entrance push would precipitate
the child across my narrow room and she always ended up crouching
under my table exactly like a cowed little dog. She would stay there
– quite still and silent – until her mother came to fetch her, saying
'Now then, come on out of there!', as she hauled her out by one arm.
No matter what I said or offered her, she made no move at all,
although this waiting time went on for many weeks. I always chatted
to her as I sat at my table, but there was no response at all.

You might well ask, 'Why didn't you do something?' The answer
is that this child had been living in a world where she was treated
like a funny little *dog* – albeit a very frightened dog; frightened not
only by the big world outside, but also of her own inner energies
which she could not express. I knew that I must not break into this
closed world she was cowering in by any imposed approach of mine,
until she might be able to open the door to me.

Most of the children I am describing here were able, eventually,
to open the door to me, provided I could wait long enough and with
unanxious patience outside. It is like the gateway into the sacred
world of the child's own soul, and the key is on the inside. We must
never pick the lock!

Waiting like this can be difficult, especially in a clinic where
pressure to get on with the job is added to the anxieties of parents,
doctors, teachers – or one's own. With Margaret I waited.

Then, one day, as I sat there quietly working at my table with the
little thing huddled paralysed as usual in a corner underneath,
suddenly I felt a sharp pain in the back of my legs and without
moving or looking I became aware that the little creature was digging
ten exceedingly sharp little nails into my flesh. I had to bear it
however, without moving or resisting, even to defend, for at last
this tiny repressed child had dared to make a relation with part of
the threatening, intolerable world around her. I said, 'That's right,

you hold on to my legs', and she did, and as soon as I dared, I very gently drew backwards and she followed, clinging, and ended up on my lap, protected. She spent many weeks completely silent, curled up in my arms, while I talked to her as to a baby, rocked her, carried her round, showed her things and never expected her to talk or act except as an infant. At long last, one day, she got down by herself and said, 'I want your dolly'. There was a doll among the toys. I gave it to her – permanently – and that doll brought her to life and to speaking.

THE FALSE SELF

If the selection process of dissociation is not stable enough, or breaks down under the impact of too heavy an environment, then we see in a child the development of a false self. The intolerable experience is banished from awareness, and this is especially true when the hostile assault comes from inside and so must be disintegrated from the surviving *part-personality* – which then becomes a false self presenting to the outside world. At worst, the whole of emotional and mental life is withdrawn like this, and goes under a lid. I often point this out to older children or adults: – '*You* are living on top of a lid, and the real *You* is imprisoned under it.' Such a one is like a changeling, born on Halloween. When this false self is established, then the real inner self is occupied in fantasy and silent observation. Experience may not impinge directly upon it, and the individual's actions are not *self-expressions*. The outside world then relates only to the false-self system.

Often this is quite inadequate, as we saw with Margaret whose presenting personality seemed barely human – 'You can't get through to her at all', as her mother told me. But when she began to dig her nails into my legs, something from her Real Self was relating to me through emotions that were real to her true inner nature. The maintenance of the false-self system often leads to mutism, stupor and physical paralysis, as we saw with Sheila, and it is significant that both Margaret and Sheila broke through their paralysis with *attacks* on me, which were not repulsed. Because the release when it comes is usually relatively fierce or aggressive, it is absolutely essential that we – the adults in charge – should not force a release, or even invite it, and of course should not stop it when it begins. I can't emphasize this too much, for it is usually the *sine qua non* of successful treatment, or the slamming of the door if neglected.

The great danger here for me is that of my having theories, ideas, expectations and interpretations of what is going on *inside* the silent child. Having interpretations or giving them is at best a tricky business, and at worst fools the therapist more than the patient! With children it is very often the fatal blow which shoots the bolts against the interference in the tiny, timid movement. And this is equally true whether the intervention is accurate or not. It is the therapist's penetrative movement which is traumatic. (See also the story of 'Pax', Chapter 5, 'Depression'.)

The Autistic Climate

Lack of sympathy and coldness of feelings often accompany the autistic state. Such a child will appear to have no feelings, perhaps no recognition of you as a person. He will walk over you, or bump into you – or other objects – without seeming to register that he might be hurting you or, for that matter, himself, either. In extreme cases there is no response at all; no words, no movement, no smiles, no tears – stony stillness only. Nothing comes to meet you; your good intentions and *gifts* and your overtures all produce only frozen indifference. It is easy to turn away oneself, disappointed and hurt, even outraged in one's own feelings. Someone described this as 'experiencing only petrified intestines' in the other person, when within oneself you have 'yearning bowels'. It seems to me as if a child in this state has to *de-soul* everything – as though any soul contact were dangerous. It would let something in, and something might also go out. There have been two kinds of 'entry' which I have found successful. Most often – especially with a child – it is through contact with the *whole* body, as with a baby. Another way with some adults has been through intellectual contact. This can go on while all feeling is completely shut down under the lid! This is hard for me to sustain, because my 'lid' covering feelings doesn't work very well!

Lack of Speech

Mutism is common and may be partial or total. A chronic and serious degree of mutism is a sign of much difficulty ahead in treatment, but a child who has begun to talk, who has retreated for any of the reasons we have discussed, will be more likely to recover. Stammering sometimes compounds the need for silence. The stammerer is often preoccupied with his need to *keep things in*, and not to risk letting things go out of him. Perhaps it is relevant here to mention the asthmatic spasm which seems to be concerned with holding the breath in and paralysing the exhalation.

With these very withdrawn children, some are compliant and others – especially very young ones – are quite unable to leave their mothers and spend time alone in a room with a stranger. Here again, it is the child's needs which must be recognized and met totally – irrespective of therapeutic goals, 'waste of time', therapist's anxiety, pressures from parents, doctors, etc. I have gone through the whole of a successful treatment with the child sitting on his mother's lap during every interview, over at least a year. And more than once I have conducted satisfactory sessions in the public waiting rooms with other patients coming and going and waiting there. The child could tolerate the somewhat more familiar world of children buzzing round, but was terrified to enter solo into *my world*. This acceptance of the child *as he is* – for a long time, rather than a promise of acceptance if he will change – can mean the difference between his ultimately daring to relate to me – or not – and then through me to the outside world more generally.

USING SPECIAL ABILITIES

A mute, autistic child sometimes has a special ability which can be fostered. Ability to manipulate manually such things as gadgets, wheels or tools is occasionally advanced. Possibly this capacity develops because such things are predictable, unresponsive and can be controlled. One older boy of seventeen who never learned to speak or read and made no contact with people, nevertheless taught himself to take clocks to pieces, oil, clean and reassemble them satisfactorily. He was completely absorbed while doing it and showed every sign of feeling secure, but if I tried to talk to him personally, he became fearful and agitated. If I talked to the clock, however, he was happy.

If such a child can treat people as objects instead of *persons*, he may seem more secure and less threatened by a challenge he cannot manage. If he talks at all he may refer to a person or a part of himself as '*it*', like a boy who seemed to need to lower my status as a personality (to cope with me), and thereby to raise his own. He always referred to me as '*it*' and himself as '*he*'. He had a personal pronoun for himself but a more impersonal one for me. He wanted to demand biscuits when he came to see me because I had provided some at first, and if they were not there, he would sulk in a corner and mutter 'IT did have some biscuits, IT did!' When I did not respond he would get angry and whine loudly – but not to me – 'HE wants a biscuit!' Another child would refer to parts of me like that also, calling my hands or eyes 'THEY'; especially my eyes, from which he would retreat saying, 'THEY are angry', or 'Take them away', but never 'Your eyes'.

SILENT STEPHEN

Seven-year-old Stephen came to the clinic mute and assessed as 'psychotic'. He had not spoken since five and a half. Apparently he had been quite normal until reading started at school. He missed a few crucial early weeks through measles, and when he returned and was faced with *catching up* he completely shut up inside himself and stopped speaking or responding to people at all. Occasionally he would wander, but without any goal – just aimless, vague wandering.

This was another case where I took up my favourite position of lying on the floor. I like to get as low as possible with these very insecure children. So I lay across the floor of my very narrow room playing quiet marbles all by myself, in such a position that Stephen could not move from one end of the room, where the toy cupboard was, to the other end, where the sand tray was, without stepping over me. This didn't daunt his style at all. He regarded me exactly as you would regard a mat on the floor, with one difference: he stepped *over* me every time on his regular journeys, carrying toys with both hands, but he didn't appear to look at me at all, except that he never knocked me once. Occasionally I would look round and say 'Hello!', or make some comment. This evoked no response at all, except that it made him anxious if I tried to contact him. Weeks went by and still we played this unchanging game. He wasn't anxious as long as I didn't speak to him or show him that I expected to be treated as anything more than a mat on the floor.

The only thing which could be seen to develop was that at the beginning he always stepped over my feet when travelling backwards and forwards from cupboard to sand tray. This lasted for some time, and then I noticed out of the corner of my 'unconcerned' eye that he was stepping over my legs at knee level. Gradually he came up my body as the weeks went by, feet, knees, thighs, waist, chest and then shoulders. Even with this width and with both hands full of toys, he never once touched my body at all with his feet. In fact, he made no physical contact, and if I held out my hand when he came or went, he ignored it and faded away like a wraith. If you went to put your arm around his shoulder you would find he wasn't there, he had used the air to waft himself just that fraction of an inch away, much like a bird who will let you approach to within that fraction but no more!

Then suddenly one day, after he had made his many journeys stepping over the *mat, the object, the it,* he stepped over me at neck level, but instead of continuing to the sand tray with his toys as usual, he stopped, stood still with his back to me for a time, and then turned, still holding the toys in both hands, stooped down and kissed the top of my head. At this I raised my head and looked at him and said 'Ooh, nice!' He then turned away and took the toys to the tray, but he came back and stood near me looking down at me, which he had never done before. I continued to look at him without moving, and I can only say that the feeling was of love. Then his lips began to tremble and to form, and gazing at me like a creature from the sea, slowly and softly he spoke to me one word: 'YOU'.

He had recognized me, he now dared to recognize me as a *person*. 'Ordinary' therapy was now possible and very rapid.

PAULINE

Another example of a thrilling breakthrough from the Autistic prison concerned sixteen-year-old Pauline, who had been away from Grammar School for many months, apparently very ill. Doctors were puzzled by her condition, and finally diagnosed her as schizophrenic and advised psychiatric treatment in hospital. Her name was on our waiting list, however, and our vacancy was offered before the hospital appointment. It was interesting that the doctors agreed she could try psychology at the Clinic, saying 'Yes, while you are waiting for the hospital – it won't do any good I'm afraid, but it won't do any harm!' (1947).

Pauline was brought in by her mother, who told us that the girl had gone downhill for some time, and had been quite mute since her dog had been killed in an accident many months before. I was the first to see Pauline at the Clinic and I was supposed to take an Intelligence Test. I knew only that she couldn't speak, and was called 'psychotic'. She could not speak a word to me, but only gazed with a glassy stare of terror. As she was sixteen and from a Grammar School, I gently explained that her mother had told me she found talking difficult, but I didn't require her to talk to me, so would she like to see some of the exercises we did, and if there was anything she could take part in by writing, etc., that would satisfy me. She nodded ever so slightly and I began to show her how tests were constructed for very young children; e.g. different kinds of memory, etc. She seemed interested in all this in a dumb, heavy way, and when I began to ask her questions she wrote down short answers, or drew pictures without any difficulty. She didn't seem distressed or anxious in doing this, but acted in an automatic and mechanical way. It was all very impersonal until I praised her in a feeling way for something she had written. Emotionally I felt a change in her, and suddenly I experienced that flood of feeling in myself, almost as if entering a trance state – a sure guide with these mute children. Because of this, when it came to the next question, I didn't provide paper and pencil, but, holding the emotional responsive feeling steady, I asked her to tell the meaning of the proverb, 'A bird in the hand is worth two in the bush.' 'Pauline – could you tell me what that proverb means to you?' I waited as she gazed into the distance for a long time. At last she began to speak in a far-away, monotonous voice, rather like the voice of a totally deaf child who has learned to speak by lip-reading and has no intonation. She said: 'The birds in the bush you cannot see, and if you go up to them they fly away.' Here she paused for a long time while she seemed to be struggling with deep emotion, turned and looked at me with her deep, dark brown eyes as if seeing me for the first time. Then she continued in a warm and more lively voice – 'But the bird in your hand you can have and hold and it's nice for you.' With these last moving words, her closed door opened and she let me enter.

This all happened at the first session, and almost at once she began to talk to me. Later she described how she 'had gone back to the beginning of the world. I seem to live there all the time. I used to live with people, then there weren't any people any more. There were only animals. Then I lived with animals. I love animals, they're nice for you. Then there weren't any animals any more, my dog died. I couldn't have animals after that, and then I only lived with plants – and now the plants seem to be fading, and after that there's only the beginning of the world. I don't like the cold.' After this our sessions were like two intelligent adults talking together. She would have made a splendid therapist! She recovered very well and relatively rapidly. I insisted that she had another dog, and eventually she finished her education and became a Grammar School secretary.

SUSAN

A moving and impressive story of one of these silent children concerns Susan. She was nine and a half, and had become increasingly unhappy ever since her parents separated and her father disappeared out of her life. She had one sister, Rita, born when Susan was still a baby of fifteen months old. Rita was quite unashamedly the mother's favourite, and she spoke of Susan as 'a child I can't really get on with like I can with Rita. I just can't make her out.' Susan had stopped speaking at home and at school, and it was significant that it was the school and not her mother who pressed for something to be done.

She came to me privately and as usual I explained that I knew it was difficult for her to talk, but I didn't mind, and she could use any of the things I had as she liked. She chose drawing for which she had a special talent, so I did drawing also, and when we were tired of that, we played games – draughts, tiddly-winks, etc. If I asked a question (I was careful to use rhetorical questions), she might nod, or once or twice whisper 'Yes', but was otherwise quite mute and depressed.

After the familiar weeks of waiting, there came a day when we were playing tiddly-winks on the carpet. I got tired and said 'Susan, I'm rather tired and my back hurts. Do you mind if I sit down and rest for a few minutes – you go on if you like and I'll come back soon.' I sat down and closed my eyes. I heard a movement and was aware that she had put a cushion at my back. I said 'Oh, that *is* nice. I do love being looked after.' She smiled, and went back to the game on the floor.

Because I felt that her gift of the cushion had opened a new channel between us, I began to tell her how I thought she was so unhappy, because when Rita was born, Susan had lost that *special love* which a baby needs to have, continually. I said how often this happened, and it can feel like a terrible loss to the older baby. She went very still and hung her head, and then I said suddenly, without any thought or plan: 'You know – you will never get it now.' Feeling dreadful at what I might have done to her, I plunged in: 'Susan – you made me so happy when you put a cushion at my back, and now I want to ask you to do one more thing for me – will you try and talk to me?' She kept very still, and this was the following conversation:

'Who do you think looks after you when you are too little to look after yourself?'

There was a long silence, and then she sat up and looking straight ahead with a gaze which spanned a hundred years, said slowly:

'All the mummies.'
'*All* the mummies?', I asked.
'Yes – all the mummies in the world.'
'Do you mean that all the mummies in the world could look after one little girl?'
'No – I think *we* mean that I shall get it when I turn into a woman.'

And in such a magnificent way this silent, dreaming child approached me through her recognition of the inspiration of that great universal Mother Archetype – 'All the Mummies in the World.'

The family soon moved away and I lost touch. Fourteen years later I was given a message by a relative who had returned to London from a visit to Canada where Susan – now married – was living. 'If you see Mrs Jeffrey in London, tell her I have now got what I always wanted – my first baby has just been born.' Why don't we listen when the children speak, why don't we listen when a child can't speak? And bow before the majesty of the innocently weak.

3

CHILDREN THINKING

Nothing is more fascinating than evidence of the way in which children – even babies – think. Before an infant has acquired any degree of verbal language, the thinking process seems to focus on action, using memory and foresight purposefully to develop favourable practical skills. Then intelligence starts to make adaptation to variations of experience, and 'thinking' has begun. Naturally most of my observations were with my own children, so they all feature here.

What my own children taught me was fundamental to the development of my therapeutic work with child patients and with the child part of adults also. I would describe a child patient to one of my own children, of appropriate age, and was often startled and informed by the penetrating perception of diagnosis and treatment required, which a child could intuit. I remember a boy I was seeing in a clinic where both of us seemed completely stuck and I could not see why. When I told my son of the same age (eleven), he said passionately, 'Give him something to *do* – something to make!' and he rushed away to fetch some bits of balsa wood and tools for me to offer the boy. He was right, too, as it proved later.

ROBIN

At the age of sixteen months, my second son Robin had been put in a drop-side cot for a day sleep and I lay down on a bed across the room for a short rest. Hearing noises, I opened my eyes a slit and watched a bit of early engineering. He didn't want to go to sleep, so he stood up on the pillow and lifted one dropper catch holding up the cot side. Pushing the rail down did not work because the dropper held at the far end. Failing in this once or twice, he regarded the far catch, and scrambled over to repeat the process at that end, but saw that the first catch had dropped back into place. He then returned to the pillow, and sat down to think. After a few moments, he began to struggle with his two-pin nappy, finally getting it off over his feet. He stood up, wedged the dropper open with the wad of nappy, and

31

carefully crawled over to the far side, lifted that catch and down went the cot side. Not surprisingly, this child's later chosen career was in engineering. When Robin began to talk, he had a special way of describing Time. Any question about *when* did anything happen always brought the reply 'Yesterday today a-morrow', pronounced as one word. He had a comprehensive concept of time before a verbally expressed thought had fully formed.

I Want to be ME

At five, Robin was being pinned down by a rather persistent neighbour, known as 'Auntie'. 'Well, Robin dear, tell Auntie what you're going to be when you are a big man?' No reply. 'Going to be an engine driver or a big policeman?' No reply. The child literally had his back to a wall and stood there with tight lips. The questioning went on with hurt insistence. 'Oh well, I'm not going to talk to you if you won't tell Auntie.' At this, the child burst out, indignant at the silly adult and said with great force, 'I don't want to be *anything* – I want to be ME!'

Teachers who Learn

The same child, aged thirteen, was up before his headmaster at a boarding school, because of complaints from several teachers of inattention and unacceptable work in their subjects. After a sharp criticism, the Head asked the boy for his own views, and after being assured that he could say what he liked, he continued, 'Very well then, there are only two teachers in your school who can really teach, and I get on all right with them.' The Head agreed that those two were excellent teachers, but asked the boy why he thought so. The reply was: 'Because those two teachers learn from us, and I can learn anything from a teacher who learns from me.' (This was told me privately by the Headmaster.)

SALLY

My daughter, Sally, was two and a half when I was pushing her in an open pram in an unfamiliar country road where we had just arrived for a holiday. The scene was quite new to her and when we were overtaken by a girl in jodhpurs, she stared intently after the girl until she had gone into the distance. She then turned to me, and asked almost accusingly – 'What's that lady got trousers for?' This was before the advent of jeans, and what interested me was the adverbial phrase enquiring about a purpose in the lady's dress. 'What for?'

'THAT MAN JUNG'

I had written to Jung for advice about a problem I was finding with several of my women patients. I had a lengthy reply from Jung, and on an impulse I gave it to my sixteen-year-old daughter to read. She said, 'That man Jung must be very clever, because what he says is just what you always leave out. You see, he means that you have to find it in yourself, and perhaps you can't. Mind you, it's alright coming from a man, but I wouldn't like it to be what you think, and I don't think like that myself, and he's a man, so if you put us together it makes sense.' I was struck by her natural thinking which perceived the value in balancing the opposite viewpoints of men and women. All three of us were involved in observing this problem and Jung had said he had 'found the same difficulty with his patients, and could give no general answer'. Also, what was very valuable to me, was how she perceived what Jung said. I 'had to find it in myself, and *perhaps you can't.*'

'VISIONS AND THINGS'

Michael was nine when he told me that he had been thinking, 'Oh, about all sorts of things, about this world and what it really is, and how it got here and where it's going.' (Pause for breath.) 'Then another thing I've been thinking is that when a child is born into this world, it's much more of an end than a beginning.' 'How do you mean, an end?', I asked. 'Well, it seems more important somehow before you're born, and a longer time.' 'Do you remember being born then?' 'Oh yes, of course I do. I should have thought everybody would remember that.' This did not surprise me, for I have met several children who had quite vivid and individual memories of being born. He described the experience as 'being shot through a long darkness, and then there was a blinding flash of light and then I became unconscious and I stayed unconscious until I was a little boy and could understand things AGAIN'. This is a far memory carried in the body until the 'mind' forms it into thought. The child continued: 'I know all these people – like scientists – are trying to find out about all these things, but they never will the way they are trying, like with their 'outside eyes'. They will only find it out with their 'inside eyes' and Visions and things.'

When this boy was fifteen I was apologizing to him one day for the many mistakes I felt I had made in handling him in earlier years. He listened for a while and then said, 'Why didn't you tell me this before? You have had fifteen years. I would have told you what to do.'

Many other children have told me things which expressed their own thinking, sometimes startlingly unique or related to eternal things. Susan, who is described in 'Silent Children' (Chapter 2) was such a child, when she could contact and understand the nature of the Mother Archetype – 'All the Mummies in the World'.

CHRISTOPHER

Christopher, aged nine, had been asked to leave his Preparatory School, not for behaviour – which was excellent – but because the staff said he was unteachable. 'He is simply not with us, lives as if in a trance, and we think he needs special education of some sort.' At the time I was free to offer to educate him privately for eighteen months until he was eleven. I found at once that he was highly intelligent and a very deep thinker, already almost a philosopher. It was quite clear that a boy so introverted and intuitive would find it difficult to keep up with the more superficial reality demands among the rough and tumble of a boys' Preparatory School. This is a typical conversation I had with him early on in our contact. He had been reading to me and came across the word 'wisdom'.

I asked, 'Do you know what that word means?'
'Well, I think I do, but I don't quite know how to say it.'
'Could you say what a wise man would be like?'
'A wise man? I think he could be clever.'
'Yes, he might be clever. Do you think that a wise man and a clever man are the same?'
'Oh no, no! I don't think that at all. They are not always the same – they could be the opposite.'
'How do you mean, the opposite?'

'Well, they could be the opposite because a clever man knows how to do things, but a wise man would know – a wise man would know *which things* to do.'

At eleven he entered a Public School and did very well there. The eighteen months of 'tuition', four mornings a week with this boy, was a time of sheer delight for me. The process of helping him to harness his outstanding thinking ability to use in his progressive education generally was as valuable to me as to the boy himself. His mother told me secretly that when he referred to me at home, he never used my name, but began his sentence, 'SHE said', and so on.

RETARDED THINKING

Stella was eight and mentally retarded. She had been accepted as an experiment at a fee-paying girls' secondary school, where I was working at the time, and as she could not take part in class lessons, was put in my special care, and she came round with me to whatever room I was in, and I fitted in a few simple tasks for her. One day I was invigilating a school exam, and Stella was sitting out in front of the class, facing my desk, and playing quietly by herself with some activities I had organized. She was always very quiet and obedient. I was writing a report, and suddenly wanted to underline a heading. I looked up a split second before realizing that I must not disturb the exam class, but Stella seized a ruler from among several objects on her table and held it out to me. Afterwards, I asked her how she knew it was a ruler that I wanted, and she said, 'You asked me for one.' This was by no means an isolated incident of that kind, for this mentally defective child read my practical thoughts like a book.

'I'M FED UP WITH THIS'

A five-year-old boy, Colin, was reading to me from an infant reading book, the story of the Little Red Hen, where page after page repeats: 'Who will reap the corn?', 'Who will grind the flour?', 'Who will mix my cake?', etc., etc. Each time, all the animals answer one by one in turn: 'Not I', said the dog; 'Not I', said the pig; 'Not I', said the duck; 'Not I', said the goose and so on. After faithfully ploughing through about four repetitions, Colin heaved a big sigh and said emphatically, 'Oh, I'm fed up with this. Not I said the dog, pig, duck and goose!'

UNCONSCIOUS THINKING

Brian, aged six, was referred to the Clinic because of a fear of the dark. In daylight he seemed a happy, healthy child with no worries, but the fear came on at twilight. The anxiety was not mentioned during our first few sessions, until confidence had been established in me and the situation. Then one day I asked Brian to play by himself for a bit while I 'had a rest'. This was a method I found very useful with some children. It had two functions. First, it was a challenge to the child to use independence, and second, it provided an opportunity for him/her to use a caring function and react to a 'weakness' or need in me – the adult. Brian went to the window of my narrow room which was used as an ophthalmic dark room. Playing with the black blind, he got it caught under the catches at the bottom and found the room was in complete darkness. In a panic he shouted, 'Put it up. Put it up.' I didn't move but called to him to come over to me. He stumbled across and fell on my lap trembling and hiding his head under my arm. Our conversation was as follows:

'Oh, you *are* frightened, aren't you? Something over there has scared you such a lot ... .' 'I wonder what that was?', etc.
Brian, hesitantly: 'Are – aren't you frightened?'
'Well, when I was a little girl your age, I used to be very frightened by things like that.'
Brian, after a pause: 'Are you frightened now?'
'Well, I used to be, like you, but I'm not frightened now.'
'How – did – you – get – not – frightened – any – more?'

After this question we entered a dimension of unconscious thought and we talked for a very long time, it seemed like centuries, sitting there together in the darkness. The language we spoke must have been far back in the history of Time. Surely our thinking was at a remote level as we talked of those eternal things which we no longer need to fear. Not a single word of this remained in my conscious memory. Eventually Brian got down, and by himself went to the darkened window. He then commanded me to come there to him and show him how to unhook the blind. Then, in an almost adult voice he said, 'Now, you go and have your rest.' When I was settled he deliberately pulled down the blind, clicked it shut, and put us in complete darkness again. Then with a ringing confidence he shouted, 'Are you frightened?'

This was an exceptional case, for such a wholesale improvement in the child's chronic fear seemed to take place suddenly in a single hour. In addition, the problem of fear of the dark was not discussed or spelt out for him, but together we entered a dimension of awareness below the level of ordinary consciousness. That is why I had no memory of what we said. Brian himself led me on by a sequence of questions, just as he began it with the query, 'How did you get not frightened any more?' To re-experience the fear and link it up with my similar experience as a child, began the process. It was a new thing for him to do this while he was held on my lap – physically protected, guided mentally, and related emotionally to the Mother symbol I was representing.

Although so short, this was the kind of therapy he could best make use of. He was a very intelligent child with a great capacity for deep and intuitive thought – truly a 'thinking child'. Although I saw him after that for only two or three months, he went from strength to strength and the darkness fear faded away.

4

FEAR AND ANXIETY

'What is it?', I asked a boy of thirteen who had told me he came to
see me because 'the Doc says I've got anxiety'. After a moment's
pondering he replied, 'Well, I guess this anxiety stuff is a sort of fear,
when you don't know what you are afraid of – because I don't, and
I can't find out.'

In this chapter, I will describe examples of the 'anxiety state', so
aptly diagnosed by the boy as fear when you don't know what is
feared. The cause is so remote from consciousness that effective
measures to deal with it often prove difficult to discover. The 'fear
alert' then remains permanently in action, maintaining an abnormal
state of readiness also in the physical body with all the familiar
symptoms of jittery nerves, heart problems, high blood pressure,
tension and all kinds of illnesses and disabilities.

FEAR AT THE COLLECTIVE LEVEL

With this boy – and with many similar cases – the fears causing the
anxiety symptoms are rooted deeply in the Collective Unconscious
– that primitive instinctive level which we share with all living
creatures. The language which these complexes speak is often
mystical, archaic, or expressed in metaphor, in dream and vision,
or in Art. These expressions may reach far back in time beyond our
historical ancestry. Some of the people whose experience at this
depth has been so impressive and fascinating to me, have been
children. Therapeutic endeavour with a child at this level demands
the utmost care, for a child cannot carry such collective weight, and
in therapy we try to lift the burden of responsibility from him. The
following story illustrates such a depth of fear in a little boy, and
how it was resolved.

GEORGE

Neither children nor adults can put into words these deep roots of
their anxiety. The original threat will be projected on to a 'hook';

38

that is, something in present experience which is recognizable to the conscious mind. George, who was only six years old, projected his archaic fear on to a 'hook', an actual event which was in his own life experience, but pre-birth, and so after birth he had to re-project it from there, on to 'hooks' in the reality life of a six year old.

George was brought to me suffering from severe anxiety, continual nightmares and sleep-walking, which was generally sleep-crawling on hands and knees, head first. He could never describe any of these night terrors, and became panic-stricken if pressed to do so. Being in a room with the door shut terrified him. Once he walked in his sleep out of the house, up the road a few doors to his grandmother's house, where he was put to bed, still asleep. (The parents were informed.) It was because he was in such a state of terror on waking in a strange bed, that it was decided to bring him to the Clinic.

For some time I could see that I must not yet refer to the nightmares. He liked painting and we did that and played other games until he had established some confidence in me and the situation. Then one day I said casually that I had had a rather funny dream last night, and I didn't like it very much. 'I expect you have funny dreams sometimes, like me?' Rattling on in that way I eventually got a nod and a quick return to the painting. Another day I mentioned it again, with the query, could he tell me one of his dreams. He said he couldn't, but when I suggested he might paint a dream, he produced this striking picture (see plate 1). He said it was a bombed building, and the roof was falling in. The only way out was through the little tunnel on the right, head first on hands and knees. 'But you couldn't go that way because a strong wind (painted white) was blowing you back.' Then I said, 'What about this back wall?' (This was the detail which I perceived intuitively as a possible clue.) The effect of this on George was startling – he said loudly, 'There's no wall there.' I said, 'But you've painted a wall haven't you?' 'No, I haven't. There's no wall there. It isn't there.' Well, if there is no wall there, could you get out that way?' This put him into a state of acute terror. He backed away across the room and shouted 'No, no. You can't get out that way. It would be dreadful to go out that way.'

The remote level of this fear showed that he needed me to accept the truth of what he was experiencing. So I said, 'Oh yes, I see, of course, you can't go out that way, but I am sure that we shall be able to get you out all right.' Gradually be became reassured before he went home.

I then saw his mother and confirmed that George's birth had been Caesarean. This can be gathered from the picture. The building he is in is suggestive of a womb, with the blocked head-first route out through the narrow tunnel. His mother told me that his birth had been much overdue and the operation was only just in time to save his life. The placenta had already largely torn away – perhaps this is the threat of the roof falling in which made it imperative that he should get out.

George had never been told anything about his birth, and his mother was astonished to learn that such an experience could have a direct effect and form a 'memory' in a baby. She was a very intelligent woman however, and readily co-operated with me in explaining the facts to George, in such a way that he could understand a reality source of his continual anxiety. The child became intensely interested and curious as his mother talked to him about it, and very soon that was enough to relieve his anxiety at the time. When that was settled, the archaic complex sank down into the unconscious. When with me, George often referred to the factual information of his birth, almost proudly, as though it gave him fame and he played it out many times with figures and scenery in the sand tray.

THE ARCHAIC COMPLEX

We can indulge in impressive fantasies regarding the significance of 'the back wall which wasn't there' in George's picture. If the building represents the womb in which he becomes imprisoned, then the wall opposite the normal exit would be the barrier to 'going out that way' – 'the dreadful way' – to be lost in regression or re-absorption. It reminded me of the re-absorbing function of the mother rabbit who eats her newly born babies when there is a threat from the human environment outside. We may well ask how such experience of pre-birth events can form into memories which are present in the mind of a child, and can be described verbally or in pictures. Michael, aged nine (Chapter 3, 'Children Thinking'), told how important 'life' had been to him before he was born, and claimed a state of awareness at that time which he called 'consciousness'. That seems right, for the memory is carried in the body itself and develops into concepts and ideas which can be put into words as a child's consciousness grows and expands.

FEAR OF DEATH AND NOT-DEATH

Another example of such deep-rooted anxiety comes from a doctor colleague with whom I was working. It had become obvious to me that he was suffering from a severe anxiety state whose source was remote from his overt experience. I think I sought instinctively to get to the bottom of it – a bad mistake on my part, as I realized later.

We were discussing fear, and I asked him suddenly:

'What is the greatest human fear?'
'Death, of course', he said.
'Is it yours?' I asked.

He now became very agitated and angry, and said:

'Yes, yes, of course it is, the same as everybody else – everybody knows that!'

He fiercely defended his opinion, and then I did something I afterwards regretted, because circumstances prevented me from protecting him. I said very slowly:

'Are you so sure whether or not your greatest fear could be the fear of not dying – everybody else has died, leaving you alone, alive in a dead world?'

The effect of this was startling. He went very white, jumped up and ran from the room in a panic. My last question had hit the origin of a remote mystical anxiety which he had been unable to bring into his consciousness or cope with in his life.

It is not possible to go into the personal application of that level of anxiety in his case. I can just add, however, that the imagined position of his being the only one alive in a dead world meant for him a punishment. He felt that he carried responsibility for a destructive pattern in human life, and lived in continual fear of retribution. This much of his strange complex I learned later, but I was not in a position to contain it for him, and it had been very irresponsible of me to stir it up.

DAVID

The life-saving purpose of fear

The story of David illustrates vividly how a state of acute terror in infancy led him to develop a habit of control which saved his life during a prisoner of war situation, in which 9800 of his fellow prisoners perished.

David was nearly two years old, sitting on a little wooden horse just outside the garden gate in a quiet suburban road. It was forbidden to go through the gate, but seeing it left accidentally ajar, he had been overwhelmed by an exciting impulse towards adventure and independence. Suddenly the whole world seemed to explode around him with screaming bells and thunderous roar as a great monster rushed towards him. It was a team of fire engines answering a call. But to David it was the end of the world, a punishment for his disobedience. So with a sudden trance-like power he lifted himself up into the sky from where he could see himself sitting on the wooden horse down below. He was already 'unconscious' and did not seem to regain consciousness until two days later. His mother had rescued him, but she said it was nearly two days before he could speak again and return to normality. As he grew older this method of withdrawal from the body became a habit which he found he could use to enable him to endure pain and exhaustion, or to escape from dangers. David became a prisoner of war in Japanese hands early after enlistment and was forced to work with 10,000 others on the notorious Burma railway construction. The conditions were horrifying, the men were starved, cruelly overworked, persecuted, and their human needs so neglected that they died in hundreds, until only 200 of the 10,000 survived. David had used his 'out-of-body trance' state to cope with the merciless destruction of those men, and from his position aloft he said he used to watch his semi-conscious emaciated body dealing with heavy materials and implements far down below. At the liberation he was brought home all but dying, and remained in hospital for three years, gradually building up a body again. He worked in therapy with me for three more years, and recovered surprisingly well, entering a career and later marriage. A very special dream early in the therapy foretold and epitomized the recovery process.

In the dream David found himself crouching on a small square of thick sheet metal floating on a stormy ocean. Monstrous roaring waves rocked the inadequate platform and the dream ended with the certain knowledge that this was the end of his life. I suggested one thing only, that he should associate to the word 'raft'. (He had not used the word himself.) He immediately dropped into the trance state and with long intermittent pauses he dreamily murmured: 'Raft – raft – rafter, a rafter in a derelict house ... naked ... rafters ... crumbling walls ... all ending ... . This was my beginning ... I have come so close to death ... now the end ...' His voice trailed off, his face became dead white and we sat there in a silent limbo for a very long time. I couldn't tell whether or not this was going to be a complete breakdown, so I waited. At last, spots of colour began to appear in his cheeks and he made slight movements as he slowly came back into his body. Gradually he sat upright and then in a strong emphatic voice he said:

'I think this end – will be the beginning.'
I said – 'Right! You can slip off that raft into your new beginning.'

That moment had the quality of a miracle, and from then on his recovery was steady and permanent.

CARRIERS

I have worked with a number of people who were suffering from continual unexplained anxiety, feelings of guilt and a burden of responsibility and dread for the future. Jung has described how years before the war he perceived a psychic condition developing in the collective psyche of the German people. Jung 'saw' it envisaged in the symbols of the dreams and unconscious fantasies of his German patients. This was the growth of a motive which led to the Second World War. The burden with which such deeply sensitive people are loaded can be very heavy, and sometimes one will break down under the consciously unrecognized load. I have called these people 'Carriers' (see Chapter 1). Fear and anxiety coming from this deep level is one of the most misunderstood of our health problems, and many serious-minded and responsible people are struggling with that level of anxiety. Recovery is possible if the individual can learn through knowledgeable research not to carry the collective burden as a heavy weight. This does not help humanity. We need to discover how and where these 'loads' of fear, guilt and responsibility can profitably be laid down. Someone, I think it was Graham Greene, suggested that such things should be 'put into the compost of the imagination', where the content can become a fertilizing agent. It is not easy to explain this intellectually, but this is one of the major tasks of therapy, for it aims to reach that central meeting place in the psyche, where all opposites can be integrated.

ROGUE FUNCTIONING

Human beings alone among all other species, have developed to a
high degree the cult of the individual, and reckon it to be one of
human society's greatest achievements. Surely, so it is, but para-
doxically, if the individual becomes too much of a maverick, then
rogue functioning can develop. 'Rogue' means 'grown away from',
and likely to lose contact with source and basic purpose. Adaptation
and choice are two unique gifts which expanding consciousness has
conferred upon humanity. We are using these abilities, however, all
the world over, in ways which take human behaviour further and
further away from fundamental purpose to miss the teleological
goals of the evolutionary pattern. Aggression is the very inadequate
name for the master instinct in all life. It is the powerful progressive
energy which drives forward all physical action and supports and
fuels all other functions. But how widely aggression has become
destructive aggressiveness for its own sake, as man chooses more
and more to adapt one individual aspect of the instinct to seize
through violence and destruction temporary goals which are
unrelated and finally antagonistic to progressive life. People,
animals, plant life, the earth's water and even the planet's air are all
threatened with such exploitation.

The same rogue functioning appears in the other central life
instinct, with its equally inadequate 'label', Sexuality. Here the one
individual element has 'grown away' and 'having sex' by whatever
trivial means becomes the short-term purpose, with instant gratifi-
cation as the momentary reward. Humanity suffers a great loss when
the activity of such a major function is limited to one unrelated
aspect. Then there is famine in those wider fulfilments, whose goals
are biological, spiritual and – what we all long for – the creative
miracle of balanced mutual love.

As well as its development in the dominance of an unintegrated
aspect of a functional pattern, as in these two instincts, the same
malfunctioning will operate in the overpowering drive of a single
group or race, in an individual religion which persecutes others
outside itself, and in each nation, with its greed for dominance and
neglect of the rights and status of others. Finally the same rogue
function seems to be growing in the human race itself, conceived
of as an individual dominant on the planet, all too careless of any
other life-forms which get in its individual way. Thus we risk to
lose the ultimate wholeness of Universal Life, and fall into the

accumulating error of becoming a collection of parts, instead of a Gestalt of Relationship.

If this is an evolutionary error of our time, is it any wonder that people who are sensitive – consciously or unconsciously – to these developments suffer a deep-seated agony and anxiety about the collective guilt and the threats to our future? But Nature will take irrevocable revenge, which was what the anxiety-ridden doctor feared, without being able to understand the origin of his anxiety.

Present day philosophies look forward, now with apprehension, now with confidence, to the evolutionary moment when enough people in the world will have reached the knowledge of these enlightenments, and are able to use it in their lives. This would fulfil a dream, and as this dream begins to come true, these purposeful anxieties will have done their job. I believe that the answer to this planet's problems will come when human consciousness develops as a fertile function of Relationship, within ourselves, with each other over the whole world, and with the Earth and the Cosmos. How long? How long, we cry. How long before the human opus completes its fulfilment? I once heard the natural scientist, Grant Watson, many years ago say, 'If only the great rush forward of human intellect and technology could pause – and wait – and turn around, and meet the steady growth of natural instinctive life – coming – up – behind ... What a meeting that would be!'

5

DEPRESSION

THE IMPOSSIBLE STANDARD

Body and Mind – that famous pair of twins – are of equal importance in diagnosis and treatment of the all-too-frequent problems of depression.

'My body feels like lead.'
'Life is not worth living.'
'I have no energy for anything.'
'My nerves are in shreds.'
'I am so depressed.'

Psychotherapy deals mainly with psychological factors. With Depression, however, I have many times found an approach through the physical body to be the only successful channel for both diagnosis and treatment. I am not talking about drugs, surgery or medical intervention, but a more subtle entry into what the body as a whole is doing, and what it is trying to achieve. It could be interpreted at this level as 'talking to the blood or comforting the DNA'. An example of this is described below concerning 'Stephanie', where the purely physical experience eventually linked up with the 'mind', and led to recovery. When she eventually perceived it for herself she said, 'This is gut knowledge'.

STEPHANIE

The story of Stephanie illustrates a severe depressive condition where the heavy complex was rooted in a serious psychological trauma in infancy, but where the whole experience had been so totally repressed and remote in the unconscious that expert psychotherapeutic treatment had failed to reach it. Stephanie was forty-five when she was sent to me. She was suffering from severe depression which had steadily worsened since her marriage ten years earlier. Later we found that it had started when she was eighteen months old. She

46

had no children, was heavily agoraphobic and couldn't be left alone or go out of the house alone, even up the garden to hang out the washing, unless someone was with her. The referring psychiatrist told me that he considered her to be *incurable*, much as he disliked the word; also that ECT or even leucotomy had been suggested, but would not do any good. With such a recommendation, I wondered what on earth I could do.

We began with simple relaxation of her physical body which was like an iron bar. To get any state of relaxation in an iron bar is always difficult, and so it was with her legs where I began. I worked in silence, with no visible movement, rather like taking a person's pulse. She often dozed. I didn't try any other method, only proposing these exercises. Very gradually, after a few weeks, there was a slight easing of the iron rigidity in one leg, which lengthened one and a half inches. I pointed this out to her and she shot up off the couch and shouted, 'Oh my God, do it with the other one!' I did, and went on to her arms and shoulders and so on. Then one day I asked her to talk about her childhood. She did not remember it, but repeated what she had been told after she was grown up, and particularly since her marriage. She had delayed that for many years with a panic fear of her ever having any children. The idea of contraception did nothing for her at all, for her fear went deeper than such an adult mechanism could reach. She thought she had been a fairly normal child at home, and at school, except for a continual and unexplained anxiety and a very low self-valuation. She said she had always felt that 'she was not a good person', and was 'afraid that she might do wrong'.

Stephanie's story was this. Remember, it was not in her conscious memory, but she repeated it like a lesson she had been told to learn. When she was eighteen months old, her mother gave birth to a second girl. Stephanie had been told that she was very distressed by this, and when she saw her mother breast-feeding the baby, she went into a state of rage, tried to tear the baby away from her mother, screaming 'Throw that away.' 'Put in dustbin.' She could not be pacified. Indeed the uncomprehending adults punished her by shutting her in a room alone, scolding her as 'a very naughty little girl *who must never touch baby again*'. But that wasn't the end of the story.

When Stephanie was nearly three years old, and the baby eighteen months, the baby died, whereupon Stephanie had a violent trauma of guilt, and for some days could not speak or eat or touch anything with her hands. All memory of this was permanently repressed, but from time to time she had this feeling that she was 'really a bad person and if left alone she might do harm'. This feeling of being below standard had persisted all her life, and a lot of her energies were paralysed. Her mysterious fear of ever having a child is obvious. If the unrelenting stress of repressed fear, anger and rage occurs in early childhood before the child has much consciousness, it cannot be coped with. Totally without any awareness of what is happening, the sufferer turns upon herself the primitive instinctive desire and need to destroy that which threatens to destroy her own life and security. Even without punishment or threats from outside, this turning of the original antagonistic impulses inwards upon herself can happen. This is because of an equally strong instinctive counter-impulse which is born of a protective function which collides with the destructive impulse and sets up guilt and conflict.

PRIMAL AGGRESSION AGAINST THE MOTHER

This is a whole subject in itself, because it does sometimes turn out to be the root of a kind of depression in adults – a root which is hidden, feared and unconsciously fought against for a whole lifetime. But it is, nevertheless, the life instinct itself. (See Chapter 7, 'Primary Aggression'.) Suffice it here for me to say that without this primal opposition against 'the Mother' no one would ever be born at all. The individual doesn't always fail to adapt this essential function into a favourable life-form of healthy independence, but if he/she does so fail, then the battle to *ex*press or *re*press it will be on, and *de*pression of essential energies will follow. With Stephanie we continued for a long time with the relaxation exercises, during which we talked continuously about the traumatic events of her early childhood. This gave her the opportunity to re-experience in her body the paralysing effect, and happily to develop gradually the function of release. Her depression lifted eventually enough for her to hold a full-time job as a secretary in the City for ten years, travelling in alone each day from outer London.

In this kind of therapeutic need, it seems as if in the beginning there was a problem, say before birth or soon afterwards. Developing life-functions face certain demands and emotional standards. The mind, and all the related systems of that awesome organism – a human being – have to find ways of responding which are the safest and least painful.

This might mean selection, inhibition, suppression, or even a regime of illness; for example, depression. Now, motorways will be established; there are roundabouts and check points. Guards stand sentinel at the synapses. Neurological pathways are monitored. Prisoners are taken and pressed down in jail! Some have life sentences. Something like this happened to Stephanie at the age of three, and such a neurosis may itself be a sort of 'healing' factor. The symptom has become the most favourable and safest form of development for that individual. So your depression – or mine – may well be your life-line – or mine.

The Influence of Guilt

A tragic example of this was a mother who lost her first child – a girl of eleven months, through an accident of the mother's carelessness. After several days of terrible guilt – when the mother would not come out of her room, or speak or eat – she suddenly emerged, having repressed her guilt, saying, 'God has shown me that He has forgiven me and so He will send me my little girl again.' She immediately started another pregnancy and prepared for the *same* baby, with pink satin ribbons festooning the house.

When the child was born, of course, it was a boy, but I have never seen a boy so much like a girl in his delicate features and general appearance. His mother refused to accept him as a boy, dressed him in petticoats and dresses, (favouring *pink*), and curled his uncut hair, until he started school at the age of five. One could say that he had tried to reach the standard demanded; that is, to become a girl, but had found it impossible.

He developed a severe depression which pushed him to a suicide attempt at the age of sixteen. At this point in his life he had started therapy with a very good child psychiatrist whom he lost, through illness, when he had been with him for *nine* months! I took over, and he had been with me for *nine* months when he was again threatened with my loss, because of limited School Health Service decisions about staffing. As soon as the boy heard this threat, he threw himself under a lorry, which managed to miss him so that he was not much hurt, and I was able to continue seeing him (also the mother). He made only a partial recovery after two years' treatment when I left the Clinic.

Guilt and Guilt Feelings

It is necessary to distinguish between *guilt* and *guilt feelings,* relating to depression or any other neurosis. These two are very different – the *guilt feelings* can be entirely psychological, not originating in anything the person has ever done, though the 'bad action' may have been a thought, if the person was old enough to form reality ideas. Stephanie was not conscious enough to understand the implications of her antagonistic feelings towards the baby. When she learned that the *wish for the dustbin* was a normal primal instinct of defence, she was able to re-forgive and re-value herself.

The opposition to the mother within the womb, quite properly in the bloodstream – so to speak – is the basic example of *guilt feelings* which in conscious life when ideas begin to form can lead to suppression, repression and depression of the separate, independent individuality. (See also Chapter 7, 'Primary Aggression'.)

Many of the people who come to see me with a problem of depression describe a state, big or small in degree, but often long-standing, where it is apparently unrelated to any obvious cause. On the contrary, people frequently say, 'I ought not to be depressed, look at what I have, my advantages in this or that, there is no reason for me to be depressed.' But in spite of this and with all the medical help and many changes of treatment the depression still remains.

Without a Cause

There was one quite wealthy woman who came to see me in 1974 asking for a 'cure' for chronic and crippling depression. She knew what had caused it. It was because she had stupidly neglected to write acceptance to some friends who had offered her a two-months' cruise in their private yacht! Then it was too late. They had gone without her and the disappointment had thrown her into deep depression again, for the umpteenth time in her life. That was her story, and she had seen numbers of doctors and psychiatrists who had all told her they could do nothing for her. She left me – quite angry – after six visits, saying that it was obvious that I was not going to produce a cure for her depression. That was twelve years ago. Last summer she turned up again. The depression was worse than ever. She knew the reason. She had sold her magnificent flat in an expensive London Square, and bought another one which she hated, and she could have had her old one back but left it too late to accept the offer. She had also neglected to accept another offer of a yachting holiday with the same friends again, and she was badly in need of a holiday and bad luck had made her miss these opportunities, and that was the cause of her depression. I told her that she was surrounded by riches and advantages, but she was making an industry of her depression, and her energies were going into that. If I could help her to redirect and re-educate her energies, I would try. She was again very angry with me and told me that obviously I did not understand a thing about her depression, and like every other doctor and therapist she had seen, (their name was Legion), I was no good, and she left! I thought, 'She will be back in another twelve years with another missed cruise, and I shall be a hundred!'

When a chronic state of depression of such a kind maintains and increases we are now entering the realm of despair, and here we find that the depression we know about sits on top of another one which we don't know about, originating from quite unconscious causes, maybe rooted in earliest experiences of pre-birth, or fed from ancestral complexes or influences. In that case I failed to hold her long enough to begin such a search.

ORIGINS FROM PRE-BIRTH INFLUENCES

Research into the science of pre-birth experience in the physical substances and processes of a human body – including what, after birth, will be called *the Mind* – is still in its infancy, compared with the vast knowledge and technology devoted to treatment of the manifold symptoms arising from it. More about this will be found in Chapter 7, 'Primary Aggression.'

OTHER PEOPLE'S BURDENS

There is a particular kind of depression where the individual is carrying a burden which does not, and never did belong to her at all. In the following case it was a child, but we often see the same thing in an adult. Where the original cause was quite unconscious and has developed into a life-long chronic state of *depression without a cause*, and therefore accompanied by guilt and more depression in the familiar vicious circle. This same principle may be operating in many cases where an individual is trying to live someone else's life or some part of it – maybe with the best and most unselfish intentions. It simply can't be done without the *depression of one's own life*. However, in this world of competition many of us may feel forced to make the attempt.

THE STORY OF PAX

An impossible standard facing a baby is illustrated in this dramatic history of Pax.

This story describes how entry into the fiercely closed world of a four-year-old child was possible. The child's name was Pax which was very significant as I will tell you later. When brought to me for the first time by both her parents, a full-scale lunch, picnic style, had been prepared, including food for me and a tablecloth. This, however, was spread on the floor of my room and sandwiches, salad, fruit and drinks placed upon it. They explained that the child must have her meal at the right time and she could not sit at the table. Hence the floor spread! All this was done by Mother, while Father tried to cope with an obviously restive and excitable little girl. The child could not speak, only make noises. She was so violent and excitable that nothing was safe, and when we tried to assemble ourselves on the floor for the picnic, she launched herself into the middle of the meal, put her head down in any food handy, lapped it up like a dog and scattered the rest with both hands, exactly as a dog will scratch earth up with its hind legs! This demonstration, which I begged the parents not to stop, was the best introduction to the problem they could have given me. I subsequently had this child examined in a neurological hospital, where after four separate days, they abandoned it, because she was so permanently excitable that she could not be sedated, not even with large quantities of drugs right up to the safety margin.

I took her on for treatment almost with my heart in my mouth, and fears for the contents of my private consulting room. In fact, I had to arrange for a quarter of an hour extra before admitting her each time, during which I removed everything in the room which could be thrown violently, broken, destroyed or converted into too great a danger. She jumped on tables, ran on them, jumped off them, climbed up the windows, hanging on the curtains with one hand and the upper ridges of the window frames with the other. She would cling up there just like a monkey, and with a shriek she would hurl herself to the floor or on to a couch if it was near enough. She didn't appear to take any notice of what was said to her most of the time, and would not sit or play with anything except to throw or break it. You couldn't get through to her as a *normal* human being at all.

Making the room as safe as I could – I had to lock the door – I took to sitting down in the middle of the floor and busying myself with some small objects in my hands and taking no notice of her at all. She got used to this and would bang about, walk into me or over me as if I were a piece of the lawn. And then suddenly one day she seemed to notice that there was something in the middle of the floor, and began walking around the outside of the almost empty room in a wide circle. Gradually she closed the circle in, watching me intently, as she had never done before, as her rounds slowly got nearer and nearer. She went round many times before coming close, and the experience was quite eerie as if some ancient mythological ritual was being enacted, as indeed it was. Then at last she was close, and after standing strangely still and quiet for many seconds, looking at me, just as though she was seeing me for the first time, (though I did not move or even look at her), she suddenly collapsed on my lap in a heap. I didn't move except to put an arm out round her back, whereupon she buried her head in the crook of my arm and fell instantly asleep. She slept for twenty minutes without moving and woke slowly and gently, gazing up at me with no desire to change this state. When finally I got up, I carried her to the window, where she stood on the window sill, still leaning against me while she rocked herself gently sideways and I kept up a murmuring of nonsense words.

After this, our interviews followed a similar pattern, but always beginning with her *false self;* that is, the violence, and entering into this different 'real' world during the sleep.

So far as my point of entry into her *'real-self world'* was concerned, I knew it happened during those twenty minutes, for I spent that time in allowing myself to drop almost into a dream state, but with a very definite purpose – I wanted to discover *what* I was holding in my arms, and I came to the very firm conclusion that it was a six-month-old baby. It sounds like a good bit of fantasy on my part, but at that level I couldn't be wrong. I know very well what my body feels like when holding a baby of different ages, and I knew that this active child would need a six-month-old breast feed when she awoke! Anyhow, this was the quality of my feelings and therefore I assessed the point at which this child had had to cope with *intolerable reality* as at *six months.* So her treatment consisted in taking her repeatedly back to that point and that age, and helping her to learn a better method of coping with these threats. At this time I knew nothing of her history or of anything that had happened at six months. It is a great advantage to me not to know, and I always avoid such knowledge if I possibly can. Otherwise I run the risk of replacing the data of experience (as the child is experiencing it), with 'models', and to do this can often block entry into the child's real self. Treatment consisted of beginning every session with the 'sleep' on my lap, and then waking up to a normal age, which gradually increased until her activity matched her chronological age.

It took Pax three years to learn fully more satisfactory methods of meeting reality and coping with it, and by that time she was seven and just holding her own in an ordinary Infants School.

The significance of the name Pax and of the six-month age-level of the original trauma was as follows:

There were three much older children in the family, and when the youngest of these was about nine the parents were quarrelling so much that the marriage began to break up. After some kind of separation, illnesses and great instability in both parents, they decided to patch things up, and in order to make it impossible to break again, the mother was persuaded – against her will – to have another child. They therefore decided to call this child *Pax* thus burdening the infant with the onus of keeping Mother and Father together. It is significant that this was Father's idea, and Mother was really very much against it, and did not feel she could cope with another (her fourth) child, and especially felt it as an attack on her individuality by a demanding husband.

The child was born and things were relatively quiet until Pax was six months old. Then the mother snapped and the marriage again broke down, both parents went into nervous breakdowns, and the little Pax was the battle-ground for them all. Thus, at six months, *Reality* had become intolerable. Pax withdrew to a world where she held a position as an irresponsible little animal.

BODY CONTACT

It was in the treatment of Pax and Stephanie where body contact proved to be the only key to discovering an entry to the buried complex, after all other methods had failed. It was this which touched the root of the patient's soma, and there initiated the recovery movement. The autistic children also (Chapter 2, 'Silent Children'), nearly all opened out the recovery channel through touch contact with part of my body, an attack or threat, or an appeal for shelter on my lap. Many younger children have entered my world with a kiss, afterwards developing a relationship from that point, following a long time of fear and resistance. The body contact with adults, as with Stephanie, is a subtle kind of language such as animals use to communicate with each other. The vital step in this kind of therapy happens when the unconscious experience begins to expand into conscious awareness – 'Gut knowledge', as Stephanie said. Then the barriers fall away and 'mind and body' enter into productive partnership. Psychotherapy has begun.

MOURNING

When contemplating the subject of evolution in my late teens, there developed a vision of death, not as an ending, but rather as an event in a limitless journey on which our planet's life is a tiny 'loopline', leaving temporarily and returning again to the main way at our Earth's 'death'.

This early vision has persisted ever since, confirming in a similar metaphor the inner knowledge of individual human death as a rhythmic metamorphosis. From this the incorruptible potential flows out and returns again to the main stream. An individual concentrate of that limitless potential has been loaned for a time to the body which you have known as me.

DEATH OF LOVED AND HATED PEOPLE

Mourning the loss through death of someone who has been closely related, involves the process of reviewing our experience of life and contact with that person. I have included 'hated' people because so many times I have heard the cry for rescue from the distress and depression from such a post-death experience. If my relationship to someone now dead has been largely negative, angry or hostile, then mourning can be especially painful, perhaps guilty and remorseful. 'If only I had behaved differently, if only I had been more under-standing, if only ... and now it is too late!' But it is not too late! Human personality is created in relationship and relationship which has also become part of me will persist wherever the other partner is – here or there, alive or dead. In this sense then, the one who has died, whether loved or not, still has a presence here with me. With that presence I can go on developing relationship, perhaps more widely loving; or, on the other hand, an understanding which can lead to compassion in the place of past negativity, hatred and resentment. There will be created a new relationship with that presence of the dead person which still lives in me.

DEATH OF YOUNG PEOPLE

What often concerns us most about individual death is the loss of loved people out of our lives. This loss and grief is greatest when the one who dies is young, perhaps a child, who then seems cheated of its future. Even if we believe that there is a meaningful future somewhere and somehow for the person after death, there is still the feeling that this death was untimely, perhaps before experiences could be enjoyed, functions fulfilled, or wrongs put right and wounds healed. Even if we are satisfied in these things, there is still our loss so heavy and grievous to those who remain.

I do not think that this aspect of mourning can be altered. We have to carry it and hopefully the vision of persisting potential will help to integrate the experience into a balanced meaning of life and death.

Let the beautiful words of John Donne sum it up for us:

> I am re-begot.
> Of absence, darknesse, death;
> things which are not.

6

FOUR PEOPLE – TWENTIETH-CENTURY METAMORPHOSIS OF MARRIAGE

'She is just like me, which is why I married her', a young man told me at his wedding thirty years ago. Ten years later he had left his 'changed wife' and married another girl who was again 'just like himself'. This marriage lasted only four years, and another relationship had started, but was soon breaking up according to the same pattern.

At this point the man came to me asking, 'What is the matter with all these women that they change so much after they are married?' I asked him, 'Do you change at all?' His reply was emphatic, 'No. I don't! Why should I?'

Therapy with him was very slow and, for me, particularly trying. He could not tolerate the slightest change in me or in any arrangements I made. It became clear that if I 'changed', he would leave. Rightly or wrongly, my feeling was that he must continue in therapy and that conditioned the course I had to take. Inevitably, although only after a prolonged and apparent stalemate, it became unbearable to me. One day I said to him, 'I can't bear this any longer. You have made me a Pillar Saint, and I just have to get down. There is no life for me up there.'

Perhaps it had not been wrong to wait, for at that moment he was able to respond to *my* need, and at last therapy could begin. Although we always had to work through heavy resistance, he never quite lost touch with the slow-growing bit of himself which had begun to want to supply the need for development in another person. The third marriage, though stormy at times, did last.

What caused the young husband to leave all his wives was his experience that each woman changed and developed herself as the years went by. The trouble was that he did not change by developing himself, so no balancing adjustments to each of the individual personalities could happen. Although therapy was so difficult, at long last the realization grew in him that the *sine qua non* of any relationship depends on the recognition and honouring of the individual singularities by one for the other. This is the great work

57

of love in any relationship. It was Alan Watts who said to me, 'Love
itself is the living and accepted experience of another person in all
his uniqueness and differences, and one is truly loved – and one
truly loves – only when one's incomparability is part of the relationship, and one experiences the other's personality as a world in
itself.'

THE FOUR PEOPLE

It has been usual in times past, to think of marriage as being a relationship between two people – a man and a woman. In fact, there
are four people involved in the partnership – two men and two
women. As long ago as 1899, Freud wrote that he could recognize
that 'four individuals were involved in every act of sexual intercourse'. There is still a need for the recognition of this principle
within all forms of relationship between men and women. As all
four live in the same house, share the same bed and are parents of
the same children, is it any wonder that problems will arise in the
dynamics and volcanics of such intimate functions and contacts?
There will be loving and hating, arguing and reconciling. There will
be dependence and rebellion, joy and despair, and above all, power
struggles between all four. If harmony is achieved, it will happen
when differences are honoured, change accepted and opposing characteristics respected.

Male and Female

How there came to be two men and two women when we see only
one of each, I expressed in this extract from a poem called
'Conjunctio' written forty years ago.

> Once in some hundred million years,
> An Eternity ago:
> For reciprocal heaven of joy,
> Or isolate hell of woe;
> Somehow, and in some place
> Fortuitous or subtly designed,
> The One Life vibrated
> With the first dim quickening of a Mind.
> *Aim* stirred the unconscious monster
> In its primordial sleep;

Begetting celestial chaos.
He burst skyward with a leap
That tore the protesting serpent
From its encincturing earth,
And wrested Man's bold significance
From woman, in a birth.
So, in that early hour,
Was mighty mischief set a-brewing ...
(C. Jeffrey)

The Physical Basis

A man is still quite different from a woman, no matter what protests are raised to the contrary in these days of 'unisex equality.' Within two months of fertilization, the differentiation becomes established in the uterus whether the developing embryo shall be male or female. Up to that time the embryo is female, but then if a Y chromosome has been donated by the sperm, the foetus begins to develop as male. Only the male sperm carries Y chromosomes, so absence of a Y will result in a dominantly female foetus.

It is interesting to note that male testes begin to produce their own hormones at this point, about two months after fertilization, while female ovaries, although fully formed do not start functioning until the sixth month of pregnancy. That is, the female 'waits – sleeping', but the male becomes active and initiating three or four times as soon. I wonder if the anxiety of women about dominance or equality would be relieved to hear that the female ovum is 85,000 times bigger than the male sperm!

Human life seems to have evolved right away from the need for the original safety-measure of reproduction where billions of male sperm are developed continuously in all sexually reproducing animals, but only a tiny proportion will ever be fruitful. The task and the journey the sperm has to make to fulfil its life-work is highly dangerous and very competitive. The chance of success is many millions to one. I have often wondered why, in higher animals and humans, there still remains such a discrepancy between male and female success in this functioning, especially as it affects the fundamental completion and satisfaction of the reproductive operation: a satisfied completion, which is sought increasingly and with so much waste of energy and substance in the male, but is based on a slow-paced rhythm in females. There is a lot to understand here

in the emotional discrepancies which stem from and accompany
these biological processes.

Characteristics Governed by Physical Factors

The male androgens cause the male embryo to grow faster, heavier
and longer than the female. His heart and lungs have greater
capacity, muscles are stronger and longer, metabolic rate is higher
and so on. This enables the male to perform heavier tasks, to run,
throw, hit and jump harder and more accurately than females can.
A man can tolerate more physical stress and exertion as his blood
carries more red cells and therefore more oxygen.

The Male Character

These innate physical structures and physiological systems of the
male, if not interfered with too much in the processes of 'civilized'
adaptation, will develop in a man typical masculine characteristics,
both in body and mind, and in styles of behaviour and relating. As
a generality, he is expected to be active, decisive and aggressive.
Thinking and intellectual activity is often a favoured function.
Present him with a problem and he will attack it directly if possible.
He will be ambitious and proud of his strength and jealous of his
sexual powers. He is continuously impelled to seek sexual satisfaction, a function which involves him in everlasting problems of
adaptation and limitation which is at the root of a large proportion
of disruptions in the marriage relationship.

The Female Character

From the female basic constitution different dominants are likely to
develop. Where the male is active, she may be more passive. Her
immediate strength is less than his, but she has a deeper capacity
for endurance and for physical and mental patience. She, the
woman, is by nature geared to loving, nurturing and protecting the
young. She is capable of great sacrifice of herself by instinct alone if
the safety of the species is threatened. Her life is founded on rhythm,
an important factor in marriage and one which is largely ignored or
abused as 'explosive sexuality' and the free for all at any time has

become the norm. Where a man uses thinking, a woman will rely on feeling and intuition and she is usually right, for she has a natural wisdom if she is free enough to trust it. These things are true in the sense of their origin in nature. In the reality of human life, our so-called civilization has taken us so far away from instinctive patterns that boys and girls and men and women face, and often lose, continual battles with conventions, cultural pressures, economic necessities, mechanical and technological interference. There have been punishments, persecutions, cruelties and all kinds of efforts to obstruct nature's way of life and force it to conform to gigantic columns of religious, social, economic and political regulations.

THE MIGHTY MISCHIEF, ANIMUS AND ANIMA

When the evolutionary decision was taken – an eternity ago – to separate the androgyny into male and female individual parts, it was purposeful and progressive. The division of labour, responsibilities and choice of appropriate organs and functions all enhanced and expanded efficiency and economy of effort. As the sharing of activities developed, so the characteristics and abilities of each sex were growing more and more differentiated, with anatomy and physiology becoming appropriately distinct. In human life, however, there was a momentous condition attached to this happy picture. Ironically, when the separation took place, a bit of the other was left in each one. So a man has a 'woman' within him, his *anima*, to torment, frighten and limit his maleness; or, if he can accept and value 'her' without hostility or fear, she will be an asset which will balance and temper his personality. Similarly, a woman has a 'man' in her – her *animus* – and at worst 'he' will assume active power and dominance, become strident and aggressive, so spoiling her natural femininity; or at best, he will give her strength, reason, decision and, above all, an empathic understanding of how to relate to men.

A boy of eight who had always remained silent during his parents' frequent quarrels, suddenly, one day during a row, shouted at them, 'Break it up, you two!' and looking at his father said again, 'Break it up, the two of you.' Then he turned to his mother and shouted, 'Stop it! I say stop it, the two of you.' Later he said to his mother, 'I wasn't angry with you or with Daddy, I was angry with the pair of you.' When the boy looked straight at his father and said, 'Break it up you two', it is tempting to believe that he was speaking directly to the man and his *anima*. Similarly, with his mother, he could have had a sudden intuitive perception of the two people within her personality. I began to experience this fantasy very vividly while hearing the story, for I have many times seen such a depth of insight in a child. Because children live so much in the Unconscious, their perception often reaches deep truths quite naturally and directly, where adults may be blindfolded by the sophisticated demands of consciousness.

Early in my marriage, my husband's older brother was involved in partnership in our business, and I had frequent contact with him. He was a great conversationalist and loved to argue fiercely and with total ambition to win, which he usually did. I found a lot of enjoyment in strenuous arguments with him. They were not acrimonious for we always got on very well, but my *animus* worked double-time to try and keep up my end of opinion and argument. One day, my husband, who never took part in these debates, said to me, 'I wish you wouldn't argue with him like that', and when I said 'Why not?', he replied, 'It spoils you as a woman.'

This was my first serious lesson in how and where the 'man in me' should or should not function; that is not usurping the dominant 'male' role to the spoiling of the feminine.

SEXUALITY IN MARRIAGE

The sexual relation between our Four People is the major battleground with weaponry, equipment and training assembled on all sides. For a long time our culture has consistently awarded higher valuation and practical rewards to attributes and achievements which belong to the masculine potential, whether in men or in women.

Euripides in the fifth century BC wrote a drama in which the ideal world would have no women. Men would choose male offspring only from an embryo-bank and the human race would be greatly benefited. Twenty-five centuries later, after the First World War, when I was just 21, I was told that I was 'only one among a million *surplus* women'. However, the fast growing social and economic demands on woman means that she has to stretch her energies over a multitude of tasks. A young woman nowadays must earn her living often in a full-time job, run a home, be a wife, sustain pregnancies, rear children, rush from one task to the next, doing many things at the same time. This is a special female ability which men find very useful. When my father was dying, I was in this very position –

wartime, in an ancient house miles from anywhere, with a baby, a small boy and a crippled mother to care for, with no help and no facilities, such as electricity, gas or running water etc. As I rushed from one demand to the next, always giving priority to nursing a dying man, my father said with almost his last effort, 'Oh, I'm glad I'm not a woman – their lives are so miscellaneous.'

SEXUALITY IN THE PATRIARCHAL AGE

In 1944 I was involved in a piece of research in which we sent out a questionnaire to hundreds of married women, asking them to report any degree of frigidity in sexual intercourse. We had five hundred replies and considerable or total frigidity was admitted by 485 women out of 500.

At this point a vivid memory was revived in me. When I was just married in 1925, knowing nothing whatever of sexual life (girls were carefully guarded from such knowledge in those days), I consulted a highly qualified married doctor for sexual advice. He told me firmly that I 'must avoid pleasure' in intercourse. I don't know if he knew the word 'orgasm' – I certainly didn't – and he did not use it. Astonished, I asked, 'Why, because my husband enjoys great "pleasure" in intercourse, and we think it should be mutual?' To this the doctor replied with upraised finger, 'Not for women.' And when I again queried this, he said grimly, 'It is an evil thing for a woman to allow herself this pleasure.'

In the 1944 research discussion group I remarked, 'And this will be followed in thirty years time by widespread impotence in men.' I remember still how the men in the research group tried to howl me down, but I could see it was inevitable. Women were not going to stand for this any longer after their raised status and the valuation of women's work and responsibility in wartime. And so the active aggressive power of the *animus* broke out. Women tried to become like men, pushed fiercely forward and the pendulum swung right over. 'Woman's Liberation' and the feminist culture spread with force.

Looking back at these problems in 1996, it seems to me that the widespread rise of power and striving for 'equality' and dominance in women has contributed considerably to the equally widespread and almost explosive increase in violent aggressiveness in men's behaviour over much of the world. We encounter it continually in wars and fighting, genocide, indiscriminate killing and terrorism, all now commonplace, and in the alarming proliferation of rape and killing of young women and female children.

Men have a special difficulty and dilemma now that their sexual dominance has suffered so much from the threatening power of the 'liberated female.' The normal and natural aggression of masculinity has thus become more and more 'impotent' in its habitual ways of expression, and consequently men seek to restore their aggression function in compulsive and violent forms. It was as long ago as 1959 when my newly-married daughter of twenty-one said to me one day, 'I think men have a dreadful time in this world, I wouldn't be a man for anything.'

Because men have felt under pressure to hide and suppress their feminine qualities, these will be projected on to a real woman, and here 'she' can safely be attacked, despised, hated, or loved, admired, or worshipped – without his recognizing that 'she' belongs to him and he is responsible for her behaviour and what happens to her. It is thus a prime task in therapy to help a married pair to learn how to use their contrasexual functions so that there can be real relating between them all, and Eros can come into his own. Nowadays, it often seems that we have forgotten that Eros is a god, and perhaps we sometimes seek him in the 'pep pill' and in all the paraphernalia of the porn shop and countless other tawdry and unrelated mechanisms.

The Threat of the Animus

The female revolution has become very threatening to men, and anxiety, frustration and loss of power have accompanied the crumbling away of the long-established masculine role and dominance in the patriarchal society.

No longer are the monarch, the priest or the philosopher exclusively male. Even the gender of the Deity can be naively questioned. For example, at teatime on Christmas Day, after a thoughtful silence, a little girl suddenly asked the assembled family, 'Was God ever married?' (Her mother managed to say, 'I'll tell you about it at bedtime'.)

These massive changes are much more than a strident effort of a generation of women trying to usurp men's position and advantage, or to destroy distinction between male and female bodies and personalities. More deeply rooted in Evolution's fundament is the instinctive urge towards balance and ultimate harmony. It is the feminine principle itself which is striving to become free from devaluation and repression, both in men and in women. Women are fighting for this freedom by using their masculine component – the *animus* – and this has frightened, disgusted and threatened to emasculate men. Man's feminine component – the *anima* – seems often to have been ravaged by the rising power of the 'liberated female.' Women are not happy either with their forcibly acquired dominance and many new forms of impotence have developed, in women as well as in men. There are many patterns of 'impotence', as well as in genital functioning, and many reactions to it.

A large blustering man came to see me some years ago about his wife. He wanted her 'cured'. The conversation went like this: 'I am very highly sexed. I can do it six times a night, straight off, and I need it always first thing in the morning. I've tried also in my lunch-hour – I'm my own boss' [I bet he was!] – 'so there's no problem there. But from my wife I get no response at all – nothing at all. I have tried everything but she is as cold as a fish and very reluctant … Now, will you take her on?' I said, 'Well, I will certainly see your wife, but before we can do much for her we must deal with the problem of your impotence.' 'Impotence!' he shouted. 'I've just told you – I am very powerful sexually – I can do it six times straight off ….' etc., etc. 'You are talking through your hat to call me impotent!' I then said, 'Well, why don't you use a hole in a gatepost, then you wouldn't need to bother about response?' The effect was electric; to do him justice, he was so shocked that he could not speak at all. So I said, rather gently, 'You see, if it was real sexual potency, you wouldn't need six goes a night and a repeat in the morning.'

I was very gentle with him after this, which gave his 'inner woman' encouragement to develop her influence and to balance his confused and desperately impotent maleness.

The fading ability in men to restore the dominant role in marriage has led to another form of impotence which affects both partners. This happens when the 'man in the woman' is stronger than the real man, her husband (or partner), and where his *anima* takes over but in a negative way – weak, moody and masochistic. This leads to a situation where an *animus* and an *anima* are usurping the roles of man and wife, and there is impotent awkwardness and failure in real relating.

AFTER CHILDBIRTH

Another almost universal problem still persisting in marriage appears regularly after a child is born. If the couple stay together, then they face an entirely new situation in which profound changes take place in the woman – physically, emotionally and spiritually – but not so dramatically in the man. To him physically it makes no difference at all whether or not one of the billions of sperms he continually produces and ejaculates manages to penetrate and fertilize an ovum. But to a woman's whole body-structure and every process of its economy, the fertilizing of one of her limited ova is a momentous event. She will never be the same again. The event reaches all parts of her structure, influencing all systems as they respond to the great central evolutionary imperative. If she is enabled to accept this, everything will go into a new gear. Sacrifices are made, other systems are accelerated, new demands are made on her whole biology. Her body has to tolerate stress, pain, the disruption of patterns of sleep, exercise and probably sexual habits also. At the same time there should be, happily, an increase in health and vitality. An inner and outer joy and feelings of self-value should grow and flourish.

If the Four People in the marriage are well attuned, then the husband will be able to share and enjoy her uniqueness, mentally and emotionally. Now he will be called upon to accept the changes in her, to make sacrifices and adjustments which are new to him. If he can do this and let his 'inner woman' empathize with the mother-to-be, then his status will be enhanced. Fatherhood awaits him. Unfortunately, such an ideal is not always attainable in these mechanized, materialistic times. Circumstances of stark survival, finance, workload and commitments of all kinds spoil and sabotage the happy picture. Pregnant and nursing mothers frequently have to earn a living also, and the 'single mother' is a whole new problem in itself.

The single parent family has now become a phenomenon of mushroom growth. For example, in Jamaica, eight out of ten children are born outside a marriage relationship. In the great majority it is the woman, the mother of the children who is the one parent. If there has been a marriage which has broken up then the children will experience varying degrees of the 'absent father' syndrome. Alternatively, a woman sometimes decides to bear and rear children without any commitment from their father, or perhaps more frequently, the position is imposed upon her. In either case, far reaching problems in all relationships of family life mount up, falling most heavily on the mother as she battles with the conflicting roles demanded of her, and the extra responsibilities. Not only are these extra loads in the spheres of emotional and caring functions. A parent who alone has the continual care of children is seldom able to earn a living also and the 'poverty trap' is now a grim reality. The damage to the children in this situation increases as their emotional life is thrown into conflict and dilemma, while they struggle to adapt to the demands of society and of consciousness.

MOTHERS AND FATHERS

The changes and developments in men and women when they become parents provide a vast field for observation and study. A multitude of problems for mothers and fathers accompany the event and in the present-day chaotic state of marriage, our patterns of experience seem to vary almost daily, like the shaking of a kaleidoscope. A continuing serial would be required to record it all, so I will not attempt to begin it here, except to say that to woman, motherhood is fundamentally stable and straightforward, and therefore essentially unproblematic. On the other hand, for a man to become a father in physical reality does not confer on him a basic natural ability to adapt his personality to the role demanded from him. Unfortunately, in this respect, fathers have the greater problem with less native capacity to adapt to it.

THERAPY WITH MARRIED PARTNERS

Although marriage does not remain undisrupted for very long in these revolutionary days, the coming together and mating of a man and a woman still remains an evolutionary imperative, at least until test-tube fertilization and laboratory reproduction become the norm. Therapeutic work with a 'married' person's problems must be the most common situation in practice, and success or failure in the endeavour varies considerably. The purpose of therapy is first to bring about a reconciliation in the relationship, provided there is basic willingness and the honest motivation for this. Alternatively, and more frequently nowadays, it may become clear that to continue the marriage would be striving towards unreal or impossible goals, demanding wasteful sacrifice of individual potential. Then therapy is devoted to assist and support the separation process with as little damage and bitterness as possible.

The Fifth Position

Sometimes I have chosen to see a married couple who are at war with each other, where he and she come together and I sit between them. So I have two people on either side of me – a man and his *anima* on one side, and a woman and her *animus* on the other. I am in the middle – number five. For the next session, they come separately and we review the events from individual viewpoints. If the right choice is made of those who are suitable for this method, it can be very rewarding and productive. If I choose unwisely, then either they blow up and leave, or I am defeated and have to bring it to an end. Usually this method works if I can sustain my position – literally in the stocks, under a continual hail of rotten eggs, bricks and stones – as projections from all four are hurled through me at each side. Then in the individual interviews, everything has to be reviewed openly. I may be accused of favouring the 'other side' or of actually being like the 'hated one', and so on.

This manoeuvre cannot succeed unless there is serious and sustained agreement from the start that there will be no secrets. It is my job to maintain this so that paranoid accusations are examined openly every time all five of us meet together. The completely different accounts of events, quarrels, and so on, given in individual sessions, are quite astonishing and this is exposed and fought out in the meeting of all five where nothing is allowed to be hidden. All this is very taxing and exhausting for me, but whenever I have been able to sustain my fifth position for long enough, and a growing honesty in the experience has begun to develop recognition and acceptance of the separate individualities of one for the other, then the battle seems worthwhile.

Eros – The God of Love

All life is motivated by Eros. Even the protoplasm is 'erotic'. This is an important realization for our Four People as they struggle to achieve a healthy balance in their relationship. Then shall the little childlike god shoot his love arrows like living bridges of communication between one and another and within those parts of us striving to relate within ourselves. Let Dryden (1935) have the last word:

> 'He raised a mortal to the skies,
> She drew an angel down.'

Theories, like all living things, develop through a process of meta-morphosis, involving de-integration, often reversal, similar to the concept of enantiodromia described by Heraclitus, (the principle of one thing becoming its opposite). There is no finite goal to this process, for as the opposites meet, the exchange of their content and qualities becomes the building material for the new construction. The timescale of enantiodromia can vary from a few hours to many million years, as perceived by the clock concept unique to human consciousness. According to this, we might say, 'What is true in the morning, will by the evening have become a lie.'

In this chapter, the description of the relationship between man and woman has derived mainly from my own experience and obser-vation during the first half of almost one hundred years of my lifetime. Much of it may seem incredible to the generation of my grandchildren, whose present ages range from twenty-one to thirty-seven. They are involved in the deconstruction of many established cultural forms, marriage among them. I may not see in conscious-ness the reconstruction and replacement of the marriage institution, but I have a shadowed image of the moving form of that next structure.

In the beginning there was Androgyny. From this were born separate Male and Female partners. Male dominance and priority developed and was maintained by evolutionary fear. The extreme form of this became a Misogyny, which initiated the rise of its opposite – Feminism.

Now my half-light visionary anticipation of the next structure is rich and expanding in my deeper awareness.

7

PRIMARY AGGRESSION AND
MORPHO-GENETIC RESONANCE

Many problems require therapy to explore first into the quality and influence of pre-birth life during the nine months of pregnancy, and second, into those profound memory echoes in the genetic substance of our bodies which Sheldrake writes of as 'Morpho-genetic Resonance'. The child (described in Chapter 3), who remembered the time before he was born as a longer time and more important, had a very distinct memory akin to instinctive patterns which govern our behaviour. One of the meditation subjects of a Zen monk is to concentrate the mind on 'Who was I before I was born?'

GENETIC MEMORY

Much has been said and experimented with concerning birth traumas, Re-birthing, the Primal Scream, and so on, especially as these things affect later neurotic or psychotic states. The limitless range of pre-birth experience stored in the genetic substance of the physical body, is a kind of racial memory which is laid down at developmental levels, rather like the rings in a tree trunk. Such ideas as the Akashic Records, Paul Soloman's 'Hall of Records', Jung's theory of Archetypes and various concepts like Reincarnation, all seem to belong to the same symbolism. This inheritance of form in animals and plants enables that primitive creature hiding in coloured sand to change in a moment the size and shape and colour of the spots on its back to match the elements of a differently constituted sand, as he is transferred from one location to another.

The time it has taken a developing species to accumulate and store such *knowledge* and memory, can be many millions of years, so it is no wonder the boy thought it had been 'a long time'. The *knowledge* which is recognized as being experience before birth is present in the physical personality – the original Self. There is a disruption of this at birth – an earthquake takes place. That experiential knowledge reaches the level of thought-form later, when

70

consciousness has developed. As the child said, 'I stayed unconscious until I was a little boy'. The Eskimo Shaman says he 'thinks with his entire body'.

I used to do a good deal of Intelligence Testing for the Education Service, and frequently I had great difficulty in refraining from giving the child the correct answer to a question or task, simply by allowing the form of the answer to occupy a *place* in my consciousness. Indeed, if I felt this happening I had to turn my whole body away from the child, or even move my chair to a distance in order to ensure a valid result. I am not consciously controlling what is going on in these moments, but insofar as I have ever experienced telepathy, clairvoyance, absent healing, meditation and related states, it seems to me to be very similar. The medium feels very definitely the physical body itself, especially in absent healing. This fits into the study of depression when a depressed person is carrying a burden which does not belong to him at all – someone else's fear, someone else's guilt, someone else's suffering or, heavier still, the plight of those sensitive individuals who carry more than their share of collective guilt or fear, or perhaps world sorrows and suffering.

Florence, a young married woman in her early thirties came to see me some time ago feeling too hopeless and unhappy to go on. She had a most helpful husband, a very adequate lifestyle, and two intelligent, well behaved little boys. Her interviews were filled with distressing accounts of the ways in which she said she was 'A complete failure – hopeless – useless. My family would be better off without me.' Her greatest continual fear was that she would completely ruin her children's lives.

Her family maintained a strict order, where the chief goal in life was perfection. The persona and acceptable 'success' were the most important, together with academic standards, high-class occupation and so on. Her activities as a child were chosen for her, as were school subjects, training, type of career, and so on. For many generations back, the individual personalities of many members of this large group have been held rigidly within a kind of ethical prison, fenced round with a huge judiciary which allows little freedom of choice in development, achievement, motive or conduct.

During a considerable time of therapy, Florence expressed continuously her feeling of total inferiority. 'I am going down all the time and dragging the family with me. I was damaged beyond repair as a child. Everything is all my fault.' Her bottled up anger and aggression eventually explodes in a volcano of rage at the children, at her mother and most destructive of all, at herself. We have gone through this countless times, she knows intellectually where it comes from, how untrue it is that she herself is so 'bad', and the cause of it all. But the judge is on her own shoulders, and as Sheldrake would say, morpho-genetic within her. Conscious talking and explanation have not reached the source, literally in the 'physical mind'. For almost a year the therapeutic work with Florence seemed largely at a standstill. I think such a situation could have become boring and frustrating had it not been for her quite dynamic dreams, which she frequently told me. Here is an example.

'I did dream last night. I was playing with the other children in a little garden surrounded by a very high, thick hedge. It was the garden of a mound. Then I went through a door into a hospital, I walked down a corridor meeting a lot of doctors in white coats and something happened with them, but I can't remember what that was. Then I came out again into the garden and was terrified to hear marching soldiers all carrying long staves. I knew they were coming to get me, and I tried to hide in the great thick hedge.' End of dream.

Me: 'You said "playing with the other children". Were you a child in the dream?'

F: 'Yes, I was.'

Me: 'What is a "mound"?'

F: 'Where the ancestors are buried.'

Me: 'What is a hospital for?'

F: 'To make you better.'

Me: 'If you were ill or hurt as a child, what would you do?'

F: 'Go to Mummy to make me better.'

Me: 'Were you hurt while playing in the dream?'

F: 'No, I don't think so.'

Me: 'Why would you go to the hospital or to Mummy?'

F: 'I think something had gone wrong while I was playing, and I had to go to have it put right.'

Me: 'So what were the soldiers going to do to you?'

F: Put me in prison – or worse – in a dungeon or something, or execute me.'

Me: 'Why long staves?'

F: 'Oh, they were soldiers of centuries ago.'

In this way Florence interpreted her own dream, and it will be possible now for her conscious mind to link up with the morpho-genetic reality which had set up and maintained the great prison in which she and past generations of ancestors had lived. I think she will now be able to break the chain – her life opus. Subsequent dreams during the following year increasingly expressed the freeing of her own individual potential. When this was near enough to consciousness, I took the risk of deliberately organizing a direct challenge in the frequency of interviews. What I did not know was that simultaneously straightforward circumstances in her family life had offered her another challenge to shoulder more positive responsibility. Her releasing potential is reacting quite courageously and effectively to both these demands, and this is proving to be productive and rewarding for her in the therapeutic work.

Another example of the heavy influence of ancestral experience was from a middle-aged man who told me he was beginning to realize that many of his present-day and life-long thoughts, ideas, opinions and judgements were those of his father, grandfather, and even of his great-grandfather! His voice trailed off here, his body seemed to retreat and the look on his face was as if he had gone away somewhere – a long way, a long time. Such incarnated echoes, especially if they are judgemental, are likely to hold back the progressive energies and hamper an individual in the living of 'his own' life, unless their origin is recognized and understood, and valued relatively. This man's energy was heavy and dragged down physically and emotionally, and intellectual understanding of it had not helped. The repeated body experience each time he went into that trance-like state gradually lifted the atavistic load.

A single human body is woven into the Universal, and the Collective Unconscious – akin to the idea that the whole universe may be like a single hologram, with the information about all of it encapsulated in every part of it. This would be the contemporary echo of the ancients' claim that there is one common flow, the oneness of the Universe in all its parts. Jung's description is of the Archetypes as 'living dispositions, ideas in the Platonic sense, that "perform" and constantly influence our thoughts and feelings and actions – the psychic residue of our evolutionary development, accumulated experiences, repeated perhaps over countless generations. This is the storehouse of latent memory traces inherited from one's ancestral past.'

In studies of serious crime some time ago, the question arose whether we are born in chains, or is a punitive environment life-sentence enough. The suggestion of 'wrongness', naughtiness and mental inferiority still clings to the left-handed child. As late as the 1960s for example, I was treating adolescent children whose problem in development was traced to confusion and humiliation over their left-hand adaptation.

Scientific research during the last thirty years has expanded and accelerated so much that past assumptions give way to new theories and even reversals, almost daily.

During 1994 I have been involved in studying the type of education and training needed in cases of a particular disability suffered by children born with an abnormal ratio of x and y chromosomes. These children are boys and the condition is genetic and irreversible. Serious imbalance in physical and mental development is inevitable and the mental profile is so inconsistent that it is very difficult to assess an intelligence quotient. Physically they grow large and tall, but movement is uncoordinated and often ineffective. One boy I saw, aged eight, had a mechanical reading age of nine, but could not comprehend or recall what he had read. A major result of the chromosome imbalance is that physical aggression cannot be controlled or usefully directed. They are unable to integrate socially and lack of relating, frustration, constant failure and humiliation is their lot. These are tragic examples of children literally 'born in chains'. As adults, these boys are very vulnerable to being led into delinquency or crime.

A university lecturer in Psychology gave me an account of a quite distressing anxiety which generally sleeps in his subconscious, and projects out and becomes disturbingly conscious whenever he hears a report of a hanging execution. The most notable case was that of the hanging of Hanratty. For some nights leading up to the execution this man could not sleep at all, and felt as though it was he himself who was due for, and even merited, execution. He had felt this a number of times, but only in the context of hanging. It was a mysterious body experience and could not be related or traced to anything in his lifetime or that of his immediate ancestors, or in his own psychology. Although psychology with him lasted a long time, and he worked at it very intelligently, the resolving of his problem was only partial. I felt this was due in the first place to the strong dominance of intellect in his approach, and second, to my own failure to use intellect adequately in our mutual work. This made a gap between us which hampered the depth of our therapeutic endeavour.

PRIMARY AGGRESSION AND DEPRESSION

By Primary Aggression I refer here to foetal experience before birth, and its influence on later development and lifestyle. Many more women than men are treated for depression, according to statistics, and there seems to be a good deal of evidence to support the idea that the expression of anger and aggression is more tolerable in males than in females, both in society and in the individual. In so far as aggression is repressed, its energies are *de*pressed, and if this is an original imperative within the womb before birth, we have a depressive paradigm from the beginning. Before birth and for some time afterwards, hostility to the very source of life threatens the risk of annihilation, so conflict is inevitable.

I have treated several cases of anorexia in girls and women who were suffering from chronic states of depression, and who were permanently and completely repressing anger and aggression against their mothers, anger which had originated during the pregnancies. For two of these girls – one was fifteen, the other thirty – I was called in too late to follow up this quickly-discovered diagnosis, and they both died, but not before they had each made gestures of reconciliation with their mothers at a deep level, which was a comfort to themselves and to the mothers, before their lives ended. (Refer to 'Juliet' in 'The Peacock's Lifecycle' Chapter 11.) In other cases this reconciliation to the 'mother principle' has still been made, although the real mother has been dead for some or many years.

In some cases there has been no overt evidence of any antagonistic behaviour of the pregnant mothers towards the foetus, or to the pregnancy, or to the child. In fact, in two or three examples there was a close and loving attitude, and sometimes almost identification on the part of the mothers. It invariably turned out, however, that neither the mother nor the child could bear any aggression or even opposition or difference over anything, and so an essential individual independence was impossible, and the child's life as a separate person ceased. This primary aggression against 'the mother' is absolutely essential before the separation of birth can take place. This is the talent of aggression which is the hallmark of true individuality, not aggressiveness in the negative sense. It is the life instinct itself, the impulse to achieve one's birth, to oppose at the right time the *mother of a foetus* which is the closed womb. This is aggression in its basic meaning of forceful energy, whose goal is survival. The individual does sometimes fail to integrate this essential antagonism to that which holds back, so that the twin impulses towards dependence and independence will become established in a conflict which then has to be expressed or repressed. The evidence I have seen does suggest that this primary conflict resides in the physical resonance itself, and constitutes an important developmental task for the solving, in every one of us. We often see a repetition of this conflict expressing itself in the opposition of an adolescent – particularly a daughter – towards the mother, to the ideas, opinions, judgements and imperatives of the real mother, at this very special time of *second birth*, as the young adult struggles again between the *Yes and No* to independence. If this struggle, however expressed, is misunderstood, antagonized and punished, it will lead either to open rebellion and perhaps hatred, or less favourably for development, to a syndrome of depression, neurosis or physical illness.

When my daughter was about sixteen, she was coming home at weekends and quite readily took her share of housework, care of her room, and so on. Then I suggested giving her tuition in more advanced cooking, preserving and so on. She met this with surprising and emphatic resistance. We did not make an issue out of it, for neither she nor I could account for it. However, as a child she had developed her own method of tackling a puzzling problem. She would say with naive confidence, 'Oh, I shall ask for a dream to tell me what to do.' This she did over the cooking, and a day or two later she told me the dream she had 'ordered'. 'I seemed to be boxed up in a small space somewhere with masses of food spread all around. I was supposed to deal with it or eat it. I didn't want it in there and I desperately wanted to get out.' She continued: 'I know why I feel like that, because it is *your* house. If it was my own house I should want to see to the food.' We let it go at that, and four or five years later after her marriage when she had her own house, she quickly became a far more expert cook than I have ever been!

We are discussing here 'primary' aggression, such as is normal in the womb, when the time for birth arrives, and the foetus has to *break open the mother*, (the closed womb). Now this aggression can function normally and become satisfactorily adapted in early life experience. But there are, unfortunately, many factors which sabotage the normality, and increase the aggression into a powerful and lasting battle against the real mother as a person. Sometimes such factors belong to the mother herself, and her health and attitudes during pregnancy and afterwards. Sometimes they seem to stem more from the baby's innate constitution, and may defy approach and later treatment. Whichever of these alternatives seems to be controlling the experience, the environment and climate into which a child is born has the greater influence upon whether he will become a monster of hostility and rebellion, or a reasonably adapted individual. If, on the other hand, the conflict is fully understood and the rightness of its origin accepted, the result will be added strength of individuality and independence.

There is the other kind of pre-birth experience, such as I have known in a number of people (mostly women), whose mothers have themselves attempted, for one reason or another, abortion of their pregnancy, and failed to achieve it, with the pregnancy resulting in the birth of a healthy child at full term. In one or two cases the abortion had been attempted in more than one pregnancy, succeeding each time until the *failure* that was a successful birth. These mothers are themselves suffering severe conflict, and in attempting to expiate for the original hostility, they will often try to identify with the child after it is born, especially if it is a daughter, later making of her a confidante or a *greatest friend*. This kind of influence will thus deprive the child of any justification for her own basic aggression or opposition. Her individual independence will then either be surrendered, or will be fought for against the abortive process, and the impulse to strive against opposition will be grounded in the body's style. This kind of development of individual power is often very strong and permanent, and can be a very useful component of character. All the same, such a child is likely to experience in herself that conflict which opposition to the mother principle always engenders. I want to emphasize this point because it explains a considerable degree of that troubled hostility often seen explicit or implicit between a developing child or young adult, and the real mother, or perhaps some other representative of the mother principle.

There have been others who were desperately trying to carry a child full term, but kept having miscarriages. One woman who contacted me had six miscarriages, finally producing four healthy girl children over a few years, but only after the real origins of the *primary aggression* had been revealed and worked on in her therapy. Her dream before her last miscarriage, at six months, was very significant. She dreamed that her pregnant womb was inside her mother's womb, which was contracting fiercely and squeezing out the child, so that the girl's mother could give it birth and deprive her daughter of it. It is easy to see what battles were being fought out in this woman's body.

A striking example of pre-birth influence is described in the account of George (Chapter 4). It is important that this child had been evacuated and had not really experienced war conditions as being different from any other reality life, and I am reminded of a remark my seven-year-old daughter made in 1945 when she overhead an adult conversation about the imminent ending of the war. She had lived all her life in *Hell-fire Corner of Kent*, in and out of holes in the ground all day and night, and surrounded by bombs, Spitfire battles, crashing planes, doodle-bugs, gunfire and so on. She had, and could just manage, her gas mask before she was two. During our discussion about the ending of the war, she came to me looking rather puzzled and said 'Mummy, I've heard what you are talking about, does that mean that sometimes there *isn't* a war then?'

The birth experience often appears to be like a memory of a fundamental *Yes* and *No* approach to life. One man said he always felt cheated of achievement in many phases of his life – almost to an attitude of paranoia – and this complex was dissolved when it was related in consciousness to his Caesarean birth, which he felt had deprived him of the opportunity to perform his first essential act of primary aggression. It was easy to intuit his Caesarean birth, although he had never heard of it until then.

It is the final honesty of the conscious knowledge of these early experiences which can enable the child or adult to come to terms with their effect and integrate it favourably. If such factual knowledge is hidden by perhaps well-intentioned authorities, then a child's own subconscious perceptions are denied, and he will carry the depressing burden of something which he *knows*, but *must not know*. Secrets are very liable to be disruptive. It doesn't deceive a child's subconscious knowledge to hide vital truths from him, but causes a lot of guilt and anxiety.

It was said of Paracelsus that he 'touched the nerve that would resonate to our own times'. He said that the true art of medicine consists in the discovery of that which is concealed in 'things which are not'. And Pascal 150 years later was saying, 'The heart has its reasons of which Reason knows nothing.'

Not all pre-birth experiences lead to a permanent ambivalence about *being born*, or about negative and hostile aspects of the mother–child relation. Some women with a previously unexplained depression have told me that they were 'afraid to be born' lest the event would 'harm the mother'. These women were particularly close to their mothers, and this protective impulse proved to be a genuine feeling in the bones, so to speak, rather than a fantasy, and in each case there was a real reason for the hesitation. One physically tiny, fragile mother, for example, had been very nearly destroyed in a previous pregnancy, by giving birth to a twelve-pound boy – very late – so that there was very real anxiety about the chances of another confinement. In such cases there can develop in a child a lasting and powerful impulse to 'protect' the mother, probably accompanied by a developing depression of the separate individuality of the child, and later adult, and limiting any differences in ideas, lifestyle or activities generally.

A woman, who was doubtful about her physical ability to bear a child at all, adopted a month-old baby girl one month before her own child – a boy – was born. Her own child therefore experienced a foetal life which was impregnated with this fear. As an adolescent when I knew him, he confessed to me that his permanent feeling was that in some mysterious way his mother was inside him and 'spread all over him', so he couldn't ever get free from her. After therapy he told me, 'You have been the kind of mother I could get free from.' (Note – The 'break-out' boy in 'Secret Knowledge Revealed', Chapter 8.)

Bruno Bettelheim (1950) has this to say about the possible ambivalence in the relation of child to mother, based as it is on the primary aggression, when this has not become favourably adapted into development:

> Such is the importance of parents to their children, particularly the mother, that no psychological freedom is attained until the time when one has been able to make one's peace with one's parents. As long as one fails to do so, the negative feelings existing in one's unconscious keep one partially in thrall to the parents' negative feelings, (conscious or unconscious), towards oneself. Only when these inner ambivalences are resolved can one be truly free.

Not all birth experience is traumatic, hazardous or full of unadapted aggression and hostility between mother and child. Happily most pregnancies are natural and favourable, and adequately provide the growing foetus with a good basis for the future development of balanced integration between the primary aggression and individual independence. What has to become free is not just the mutuality of relationship between two people, whoever they are, but the still deeper and wider function of relationship between organism and its experienced environment, between the 'Yes and No' of all those so-called opposites which confront each other at all levels and all phases of our planet's evolution. If this freedom is not achieved naturally, for one or other of these reasons we have discussed, then hopefully the job can be done from consciousness. Then the more developed personality can understand and recognize the fundamental *rightness* of that primary aggression which seems to cause so much conflict until it is comprehended; both with the *mind* and within the resonance of the physical body, which is after all the 'house' in which we pass all our nights and days.

Plate 1 Painting by George

Plate 2 The Crinoline

Plate 3 Pair of Scales

Plate 4 The Two Ancestries

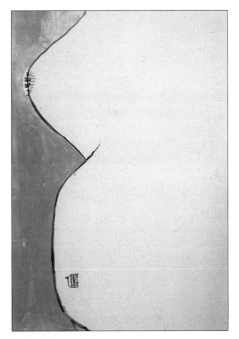

Plate 5 The Unseparated Ancestries

Plate 6 The Enemy

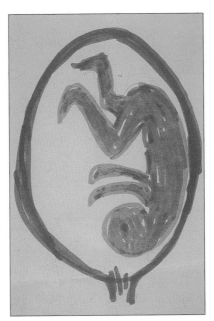

Plate 7 The Foetus

Plate 8 Pair of Steps

Plate 9 Myself

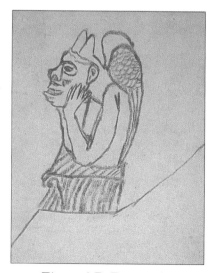

Plate 10 Gargoyle

Plate 11 Break Out

Plate 12 Inhibition

Plate 13 Final Break Out

8

SECRET KNOWLEDGE REVEALED

THE LANGUAGE OF PICTURES

The great value of the study of drawings and paintings in all kinds of therapeutic endeavour is well known, and frequently provides the key to unlock problems hitherto unsolvable. *Quod natura relinquit imperfectum, ars perficit.* What by nature is left imperfect, Art perfects.

Repressed and unknown experience and *knowledge* can project into Art form without hindrance or interference from our mental *sentinels*. The therapeutic process of interpreting and using these revelations, however, is a special task needing sensitive and patient restraint, coupled with the ability to be surprised. Acting according to what the *surprise* suggests may very well require us to reverse former tenets based on past experience and teaching. This will happen when the hidden knowledge which is emerging in Art form comes from a more remote level of the unconscious, heavily guarded perhaps from any conscious or verbal approach. Even if the drawing reveals the hidden knowledge, it may still be quite unconscious to the artist. (He may be blind to it – which will come up later in this story.)

The selected drawings shown here include pictures from children and adults. Children of all ages can usually express in drawings – more easily than adults can – a great deal of *knowledge* and wisdom which they cannot or dare not verbalize. Pictures provide a language which is safer to speak. In many of these pictures it is very clear how completely hidden and unconscious the *revelations* had been. Information compiled consciously is very different from that fundamental *knowing* which is so often lost to us in repression and inhibition.

'THE CRINOLINE' (PLATE 2)

Catherine was six; A very normal, happy little girl who was brought to my Clinic by her mother. The problem was that in the last few months this bright, happy child had almost suddenly fallen into a depressed state which had alarmed her parents and teachers, and could not be accounted for by them or by the doctors who were treating her. She was depressed, anxious and had almost given up talking. All the time she appeared frightened and watchful, but could not explain what she felt, or why she had restless, sleepless nights. The family seemed well related and the mother was quiet and adequately loving.

Catherine came in immaculately dressed in white, with lovely golden hair tied with a white ribbon. Asked what she would like to choose from my playroom, she whispered, 'Drawing'. As she didn't seem able to begin, I asked her, 'What would you like to draw?', and the answer was again in a whisper but emphatic: 'Mummy!'

This was the coloured drawing, and it completely absorbed her for the rest of the session. For a child of six, it really is a striking piece of expression, with the beautiful rainbow crinoline, and the minute torso of 'Mummy' at the top, and the two tiny feet peeping out below. I asked her if I might show such a beautiful drawing to her mother, and noticed her obvious *relief* as she eagerly agreed. She then went into another room with other children while I talked to her mother.

It doesn't need many guesses as to what Mummy was carrying under that glorious skirt! When I asked her if she was pregnant, she blushed and admitted she was – about four months.

'How long has Catherine been like this?'
'Oh, about three months or so.'
'Does she know of the pregnancy?'
'Oh no! We don't think she should be told until the baby is nearly due.'

I said, 'Well she *does* know', and showed her the drawing. I was glad to see that she also was relieved as well as astonished. All that was needed now was to explain to the mother that such momentous *knowledge* would weigh heavily on a little girl if she felt it was not right for her to know. Perhaps there was something wrong or alarming or dangerous about it, especially as it was being kept a secret? Such *feeling thoughts* would be filling the child's subconscious mind and making her anxious, watchful and depressed, as well as guilty and doubtful about her perception. Fortunately, the mother was able to understand how children need desperately to be assured that it is right for them to have such perceptions. If they can feel the honesty of their knowing, then there is no need for repression with all its attendant guilt and anxiety. She promised to tell

SECRET KNOWLEDGE REVEALED

Catherine about the baby and to share the knowledge as between partners.

I did not need to see them again, and follow-up enquiries reported all was well, and Catherine was happily helping to prepare for 'OUR new baby!'

'THE PAIR OF SCALES' (PLATE 3)

Elizabeth was twenty-nine and had come over from America to London, desperate to find help for a big problem which was upsetting her relationship with her fiancé. They had met on a skiing holiday in Switzerland where he was an instructor, fallen in love and planned to marry. He returned home to America at the season's end, and she came home to London where she worked as a secretary, to get ready to follow him. Elizabeth had lived all her life in a small hotel run by her Aunt. Both parents had died when she was twelve.

When ready she went out on the Queen Mary liner to join her fiancé and prepare for the wedding. However, whenever the subject of marriage came up, she became distressed and anxious and pleaded for delay. They were happy to be lovers, but although she always said how much she looked forward to marriage and children, it was always in the future.

'I don't feel ready somehow, something is holding me back.'

But the conflict surrounding her mysterious distress was increasing and her fiancé's tolerance was giving out, and after the situation had remained stuck for three years, he insisted that the problem must be solved. Because Elizabeth felt strongly that it could only be dealt with at home, she decided to come over and seek counsel here. To begin with, she could give no reason for her hesitation to complete the relationship in marriage, and the fear and distress was very real at any probing or discussion.

The Scales

After a time of stalemate, I asked her to put the problem on a pair of scales in a drawing. She liked painting and agreed readily. On the left the scale pan contains the snowy mountains, a chalet and the two figures skiing, some trees, the Queen Mary liner and the

American flag. On the English side, the right-hand scale pan contains only her own figure seated at a typewriter and the Union Jack. Even with the enormous weight on the American side, and the tiny bit on the English side, the scales still balance. So it was clear that the weight on the English side was unconscious and not visible. I made no comment at all about the drawing but suggested an exercise in recalling childhood memories. This was to ask her to close her eyes and just describe any memories from her childhood starting with some word I would suggest to her. The word I gave her was 'weight', and to show that she did not consciously connect it with the drawing, she asked 'which WAIT do you mean?' I said, 'It doesn't matter, try WEIGHT.'

The result was very striking. She was silent for some moments, and then began to move her body restlessly as if in pain. She put her hands on her shoulders and said dreamily:

'Oh! It feels so strange – I feel there's something pressing me down – it was like this all the time I was a little girl at home – when I was very little my body used to feel like this all the time – held down as if I had to stay like that – mustn't grow. I don't think I was unhappy because I had never felt any different, but I know it seemed as if I had somehow to stay like I was – it's strange for a child to have such feelings, isn't it? I couldn't have described it then, of course.'

When she had finished this description, I suggested we should build up a factual picture of her life at home as she remembered it and what had been told her by others.

Elizabeth's story

When Elizabeth began to tell me of her childhood, it sounded fairly normal until both parents died – from illness – when she was twelve. Up to that time, the family consisted of the parents, Elizabeth and an Aunt – her mother's sister, who always lived with them. Elizabeth had done well at school, trained as a secretary, and continued to live in the hotel which the Aunt took over when the parents died.

One bit of our conversation struck me as significant enough for me to repeat it verbatim. I had asked where she was staying in London, and she said:

'Oh, I'm staying at home with Mum.'
'But I thought you said your parents were both dead?'

'Oh yes, that's right, but I always call Auntie "Mum", ever since I can remember. I thought she was my Mum for a long time.'

'What about your real mother then?'

'Oh, she was all right, but I thought I somehow had two mothers, but Mum–Auntie – was the real one.'

'Was there any special reason why your real mother didn't mean so much to you as Auntie?'

'Yes, I think there was. When I was about two years old, I suddenly became blind and the doctors didn't seem to know why, and Mum – I mean Auntie – nursed me through it, because my parents were so busy setting up this hotel. She was splendid and she never left me night or day for a long time, so I've been told. Then my sight came back suddenly.'

'Do you remember being blind?'

'Oh no. I only have a vague memory of the day I could see – I seemed to feel like "oh here I am again!" as though I had been away somewhere. I was about two and a half then, and the first thing I saw when I had my sight was Mum, and she has always been my mother to me. *I wanted to be like her when I grew up.*'

Mother, Father and Aunt

What had happened was this. When Elizabeth was about eighteen months old, her mother's sister married, and within three weeks the 'husband' had disappeared, and it was discovered that he was already married. The Aunt refused to take any proceedings, and begged her sister to take her in. Elizabeth's mother was glad of her help with the baby while she and her husband were busy setting up the little hotel. The Aunt said:

'I shall never marry and never have my child. It would kill me to go through that again."

She then made Elizabeth her child in a total way, and a powerful symbiotic identification developed between them. It is tempting to imagine that the child's mysterious blindness was a symbol of the establishing of the secrecy surrounding the identification complex which was projected on to the child. This meant that as long as it remained unconscious (blind), she was forced to carry it and *be the same* as the aunt/mother. Then for Elizabeth also, '*It would kill me to go through a marriage*'.

This had been the problem, and when we had very carefully brought it to her conscious acceptance within the safety of therapy, she was able to return (in the Queen Mary liner), and marry her fiancé.

It was clear that this whole symbiotic complex was deeply unconscious to both Elizabeth and her aunt, for she had encouraged the
girl to marry, and had no overt objection to that, nor to her living
abroad. Such a deep-seated projection takes no account of a few
thousand miles. And how right Elizabeth was when she insisted that
she must go home to 'Mum' in London to try to uncover the cause
of the problem she was carrying.

'THE TWO ANCESTRIES' (PLATE 4)

A young medical student from the Pennines, who had dropped out
of training, came to London, took a job as a hospital porter, and
began therapy with me, to try and solve his problem of loss of
ambition and failure to go forward in his life and career. He said he
had 'A splendid childhood – my parents are great, and I always did
well at school. Everything was OK until I left home to go to college.
Then all the steam went out and I don't know what's the matter
with me.'

The painting was of a scene in a dream, and I think the verbatim
report will be the most explicit. He said:

'I was just looking at this in my dream. It's the snow-covered hills of the
Pennines where I was born. The cottage on the left is typical of my father's
ancestry. They combined a powerful intellect with intuitive abilities like
gypsies, and settled down as weavers. The cottage on the left is typical of
my mother's ancestry. She was the salt of the earth type – peasant-like and
musical. The building on the right mountain is the remains of an ancient
stockade where families and animals were protected while the men fought
invaders outside.'

I asked, 'Did you mean that the cottage on the left was typical of both
father and mother?'

His reply was startling. He became distressed and emotional.

'Yes – yes I do – I said so – *I cannot, I cannot separate the two ancestries!*'

I simply turned the picture on its side with the left cottage at the
bottom. He groaned, 'Oh my God!', and covered his face with his
hands.

'The Unseparated Ancestries' (Plate 5)

You can see that it is a picture of a pregnant woman, and his
birthplace (the cottage on the left), is still shut up in the womb where

father and mother are together. So he hasn't really managed to get himself born into individual independent life. After therapy, he did return and completed his training.

'THE ENEMY' (PLATE 6)

A forty-year-old woman entered therapy with a long strident story of her life-long experience of 'enmity from everybody'. Apparently she was antagonized by almost everyone she encountered. She had joined three separate religions, but each time felt hostility and victimization, specially directed at her, and she was forced to leave. Her words were:

'People always pick a quarrel with me. I feel everybody is my enemy. I don't start it, but it always happens.'

The picture was her expression of this situation. She is lying prone under a heavy log, and the ubiquitous 'enemy' is jumping up and down in cruel glee upon it. Both figures look alike in all respects, colour, size and shape. Our conversation about the drawing was short. I said:

'Do you see any resemblance between the two red figures?'
She flew into a rage at me. 'There you go – you are just as bad as the rest. Everything I say is always thrown back at me – it's always made out to be my fault – there's no point in my coming if that's all you can say!'
As she paused for breath, I asked: 'Did I say it was your fault?'
'Yes, you did – I've told you – it's always the same, and I can't find anybody who understands what I go through.'
'Can you remember what my question was?'
'Well, I can't remember the exact words, but I know what it meant.'
'Shall I tell you what it was?'
'OK.'
'I asked you if you could see any resemblance between the two red figures?'
'Well?'
'Well, can you?'
'Of course I can. It's a silly question – anybody can see that.'
'What is it?'
'Well, they are the same colour, the same size and the same shape, aren't they?'
'Well done! Perhaps we can have a look to see what that really means.'

Her knowledge of where the hostility came from was not really unconscious, but she was unable to accept the projection of 'the enemy' back into herself, which of course was the only place where it could be dealt with. Therapy with her was long and against fierce resistance. Many times I figured as 'the enemy', and it was quite an endurance test for me.

The Foetus (Plate 7)

A young woman presented a problem of difficult relationships with her mother and two sisters, one older and one younger. The problem was long-standing, really from birth. In quality of outward family relations there was not enough to account for the intensity of it. It was obvious, however, that manifold examples of relatively trivial acts of slight discrepancy in the treatment of the three sisters, carried projections of a much deeper experience which this highly intelligent woman had not been able to reach in consciousness.

I asked her to paint herself in her mother's womb, and this very striking picture emerged. It took some time of manoeuvring before she could actually see what is staring us in the face in the drawing. *There is no umbilical cord!*

The projected complex of emotions against her mother and her two sisters had begun in the womb. When she was conceived, her mother was breast-feeding the older sister, and even worse, when the girl herself was still being breast-fed, the mother conceived again with the younger child. So as I told her, she must have felt that she only had one third of the *total mother* so urgently needed by a foetus and a small baby. This deprivation was her real body experience at a level far remote from consciousness and accounted for the intensity of her feelings every time a relatively slight example occurred in her real life.

'Pair of Steps' (Plate 8)

A young man came into therapy for no particular reason, other than he had heard 'it was interesting – especially if you go to a woman!' He didn't describe any problem, except a vague feeling of 'never really getting anywhere – I never stick to anything for long'. I asked him to draw representations of members of his family, and this was his mother.

The drawing is a pair of steps, but one joining cord is missing and the single one connects diagonally. Also, there is no platform to stand on at the top, and both sides are laddered. I queried all these, and he said:

'That's right: nowhere to stand; no proper joining cords – they collapse if you get on them; and the two sides are the same – you go up one side and down the other, and up one side and down the other, and up one side and never get anywhere!'

So this was how he saw his mother! And if he was still relying on her for his activity and development, it is no wonder he felt he 'was not getting anywhere!' He had not yet realized that the steps he was using in his life and career were his mother's, instead of his own, and so, of course, quite out of date.

'BREAK OUT' (PLATES 9, 10, 11, 12, 13)

A boy of thirteen was referred for help with a problem of low self-esteem and general inhibition. His father was a psychiatrist and the boy's career was expected to be medical also. He was unhappy at boarding school. He began by asking if he might draw, and quite spontaneously he drew himself.

'Myself' (Plate 9)

School boy – blazer and tie – head and shoulders, all done *with a ruler*. It took him thirty-five minutes. Imagine the suppression which needed ruled lines to keep himself in order, even in a drawing. A Notre Dame gargoyle was on the window sill, and he asked permission to draw it. (Upper right-hand corner.) He wanted to try it again on another sheet.

'Gargoyle' (Plate 10)

I asked: 'What is a Gargoyle?'
He said 'It's a devil with wings.'
'Why wings?'
'They're angel's wings – you see he's half devil and half angel like us, half good and half bad.'
'Could you show him bad? He looks all good there.'

'Break Out' (Plate 11)

We both admired this as a splendid break out, as the gargoyle bursts
out of the stone in this triumphant explosion. This took about seven
minutes.

'Inhibition' (Plate 12)

At the next session, the inhibition was back in full force, and he
looked vaguely around the room for a model. This regulator clock
caught his eye, and again he took thirty-five minutes of slow,
laborious work to complete the drawing with the ruler. I began to
tease him about this, without reserve.

'So there's not going to be any break out this time. You can't do it again'
– etc., etc.

He stood this for a little while, and then said sharply: 'Well! You've asked
for it, and now you're going to get it!'

The splendid break out took only a few moments of energy.

'Final Break Out' (Plate 13)

The gargoyle devilry had broken out in force and smashed up the
clock – wheels and parts flying everywhere. This was the boy who
told me later how he felt a lot of responsibility was on his shoulders.
He said his greatest fear was that his father would die and 'I shall
have to look after my mother for the rest of MY life.'

The 'MY' is significant as he explained: 'I feel my mother is inside
me – spread all over me and I can't get free.'

Five or six years later, as he was about to enter university, he visited
me and thanked me for the help of therapy earlier. When I asked
how he thought it had helped, he said: 'You have been, for me, the
kind of mother I could get free from.'

9

IMAGE AND PROJECTION
OUR BRIGHTEST DREAMS AND OUR DARKEST NIGHTMARES

When the philosopher Berkeley tried to explain Plato's concept of sensory illusion to his students, he confessed that he could not understand it himself. Why was a tree there only when someone was looking at it? Plato's idea was an extreme specific of the nature of what we call projection – the process which does so much to shape our perception and create the images of our environment.

Projection is not something we deliberately do, either consciously or unconsciously. It happens when an image, a thought, an experience, an instinctive impulse, or any such impression proceeds outwards from the psyche of an individual, or a group or race. The outward movement is usually unconscious, perhaps instantaneous, until it is thrown or placed on a receptor in the outside, like a screen or 'hook'.

Dr H.G. Baynes (1949) wrote this, centuries after Plato:

Before the human mind had set itself to the labour of thought, myth already flowed like a natural fountain out of the unconscious. In the darkness of anything external to me I find, without recognising it as my own, an interior of psychic life that belongs to me.

CONTENT

The content of what is projected can be positive or negative, neutral, ideal or everyday, constructive or destructive, concrete or spiritual, trivial or momentous. It can carry a single thought or image or the accumulated experience of a race formed into a complex of feelings, ideas, memories, instinctive patterns in infinite variety, as the great archetypal layers of experience take formation into the myths, the religions, the philosophies and the traditions and inventions of evolving humanity.

We have become so familiar with the 'hooks' that they often veil
the wider and deeper character of what is projected on to them. This
is a pity, because in itself the hook may be quite trivial and
temporary, while what hangs on it may have momentous and eternal
value. Think for example what tremendous interest we have in
money and all that money brings to us. In the scramble about the
golden hook, how often, I wonder, do we miss what Jung called the
'gold of the personality'. On the other hand, the receptors can assume
gigantic or frightening proportions and steal the thunder from the
evolutionary movement itself. We have only to think of the monster
of the 'territorial imperative' or the looming phenomenon of quality-
selection of race reproduction in the test-tube.

The receptors which the religious instinct is projected onto all
over the world in every culture may vary, change, even die out or
suffer extinction, but the content of what is projected – that is the
potential of the religious principle itself, innate in all life – remains
to find other receptors, for it is as much an essential component of
humanity's ground of being as our lungs or our bloodstream.

As civilization develops, just as rapidly and continually, receptors
are formed and standardized, and channels created for the
primordial energies to flow in towards effective functioning in
sensory life. Rules of morality, rites and practices of formed religions,
theories of philosophy, politics and suchlike become the receptors
– often inadequate – for the eternal unmanifest and truly spiritual
energies, whose momentous value, before it is projected, we may
perceive only dimly.

We all live out the human myths, and each individual, like each
group, will project his own version of the collective knowledge as it
becomes expressed in cultural, racial and religious symbolism.
Unfortunately, it is a universal habit of human beings to remain
ignorant of our unintegrated and often archaic energies and instinctive talents. We then project them onto receptors in our
environment – often other people. These energies and their imagery
can then be experienced and believed to belong to the receptor, and
here they can be attacked, hated, despised and destroyed, or perhaps
admired, loved or worshipped.

Fundamental religious energies have often fared badly, because
the exponents of organized religion have had so much fear of the
power of archaic natural energies flowing from the basic instinctive
levels of human experience that these have been deemed to be evil;
and destructive repression has often accompanied their entry into
standardized forms. The result is always a loss of truly spiritual

nourishment, because the original energies will not flow freely into the limits of constructed form. It is like the thought in one of my husband's favourite quotations from G. Massey – 1828-1907.

> Not by appointment do we meet delight and joy.
> They heed not our expectancy,
> But round some corner in the streets of life,
> They, on a sudden, greet us with a smile.

On the other hand, some receptors of religious images are things of great beauty, and comfort and satisfy many people who still need forms of expression that are safely orthodox. Psychotherapy, therefore, has a most valuable tool with which to further development by study and integration of projected contents of the psyche. In this way the individual or group can recognize consciously the source and the original validity of what is projected, for that is what uses us and shapes our lives, our philosophies, attitudes and our behaviour.

'Good and Bad'

It is vitally necessary that projected contents which are judged to be 'bad' should be dealt with in working on development. An exceptional art teacher told his adult pupils when encouraging free individual painting, 'Don't leave out the devils, or you will find your angels have disappeared.'

CHILD'S VIEW

When I was about seven, I had been reading Genesis in a scripture lesson, I felt very doubtful about God's ability to create the whole world in six days! I said to my mother (my only teacher until I was fifteen): 'I don't see how he could get all that done in six days; how could he get all the trees and things to grow as fast as that?' (I was a very enthusiastic gardener from early childhood, and thought I knew a lot about the growth of trees and flowers!) My mother, who had the finest rapport with the minds of children, said, 'Yes, I expect it does seem impossible to you, but you see the Bible wasn't written in our language, and the word "days" didn't mean our "days", it meant a "period of time". So you see, in six periods of time I'm sure

God did give the trees and things enough time to grow.' This was
how I got my first vivid intuition of the evolutionary principle and
eternal things. My mother always talked to children like intelligent
adults.

THE HOOK

The hooks which are most useful in therapy are the ordinary
everyday receptors, which carry so many images. When a projection
hangs on a chosen hook, the hook will take on the characteristics,
the quality and the intensity of the projected image, idea, or
experience and, in so far as the projection is unconscious, the hook
will seem to have the full quality and quantity of the project added
to the hook's own identity. In this way, the hook may be experienced with an intensity and power which does not belong to it in
reality. This fact is of the greatest importance if we are studying
projections between people in therapy, or any understanding of
human relationships. (See Chapter 6, 'Four People', 'The Fifth
Position'.)

Examples

Here is a good example of a recognized straightforward projection.
Two boys from a backstreet gang were having a fierce one-sided
argument. The bigger boy was hurling abuse at the smaller one with
a stream of dirty epithets and all the horrible names he could call
him. The smaller boy said nothing until at last there was a pause.
Then he said, "Ave you done?' The bigger boy replied 'Yes, I 'ave.'
To which the smaller boy said, 'Well then – all them things wot you
said I was, *you is!*' This is what is known as 'Throwing the projection
back.'

I remember from childhood a story my mother used to tell. 'There
were two kings of neighbouring countries, King A and King B. They
had never been hostile to each other until one day King A sent a
verbal message to King B, saying, 'Send me a blue pig with a black
tail, OR ELSE ...' This sounded like a threat to King B, and he sent a
verbal reply: 'I have not got one, and IF I HAD ...' Both kings felt
threatened and went to war with their armies, fighting many heavy
battles until all were utterly defeated. On the carnage of the battle-
field, with all lost on both sides, the two kings met. King B said to
King A, 'Whatever did you mean when you said "send me a blue pig

with a black tail OR ELSE ..."?' King A replied: 'Well, of course I
meant OR ELSE one of another colour! And whatever did *you* mean
when you said, "I haven't got one, and IF I HAD ..."?' King B
answered rather sadly, 'Well I meant that IF I HAD of course I would
have sent it to you.' So let us beware when someone says, 'Well,
those may not have been your exact words, but *I know* that is what
you meant.' Successful development in therapeutic work will largely
depend upon the right use of projection, whereby the problematic
complexes and their imprisoned energies can be tempted out into
conscious recognition. Here they can be studied and located, and
then usefully integrated and come into their true value and
influence.

This is, of course, why we make so much use of dreams, drawings
and other receptors which can become concrete and visible representations of some content of an individual mind; often a heavily
repressed fear or a damaging memory , a destructive impulse or
something felt to be shameful and guilt ridden. When this is
evaluated within the safe neutrality of the therapeutic situation,
integration of it will lift the wasteful process of repression. More
deeply there will be revealed representations of those eternal myths
and truths which inhabit the collective human psyche, for these are
the true source of that spiritual nourishment which is so much
longed for by all those who can no longer be satisfied with the
traditional standardized forms of religion, philosophy, culture or
politics. (See Chapter 8, 'Secret Knowledge', and Chapter 11, 'The
Peacock's Lifecycle'.)

ALCHEMY AND ASTROLOGY

The alchemists experienced the presence of 'idea' or of 'spirit' in the
physical matter and its processes. The theory of alchemy was always
a philosophy, not a chemistry. It was the theory of projection, and
the making of gold out of lead represents the concept of trans-
forming the elementary qualities of the personality – the lead – into
the highest value in the human psyche – the gold.

In the early development of scientific thought, the dominant
images of the Unconscious – the Archetypes – were projected on to
the stars and felt to be gods. Astrology depicts this timeless
unmanifest potential of the psyche as belonging to those starry gods
in the heavens, from where they govern and influence human
personality and environment.

PROJECTION OF ILLNESS

I have cause to remember treating my first case of asthma, where
my psychological therapy nearly ended in disaster. The patient was
a boy of fifteen, who had been sent home from a boarding school,
very ill with severe asthma. I was asked to see him in a nursing home
and I visited him there twice a week for some time to deal with the
psychological side of the illness, actually the main cause. He worked
very well with me on this, as it came from an intolerable immediate
situation at the boarding school, and illness had been the only way
he could cope with it.

After some time he had worked at the therapy so well that the
asthma disappeared, and he returned to school 'cured'. After a few
weeks, however, I received an urgent call one Sunday morning from
the nursing home where the boy had been taken extremely ill with
osteomyelitis in one knee. The doctors were proposing to amputate
his leg and the boy was asking for me.

When I arrived at his bedside he said, 'I am so glad you've come
– you see I *couldn't have asthma any more* after all the work we did,
and so I had to have this instead!'

This was a severe lesson to me not to 'cure' – that is, take away a
symptom, a receptor – and neglect what is projected onto it. He
needed a hook desperately, and we then had to work very quickly
for me to take over the responsibility for the humiliating school
situations which it was essential for him to project. After that, the
immediate need for a hook disappeared, and we were able to work
on the deeper content of the problem. This was associated with a
long-standing humiliation to which the boy had been subjected
since his birth. The weight of this, when projected on to the real
school situation, was overwhelming to him. Eventually his recovery
was complete and permanent, and it was due not so much to my
therapy, but to the boy's own remarkable insight into his body and
his mind. Another very similar happening was when I visited an
asthmatic boy of fourteen in a school sanatorium. He told me, 'I was
going to have asthma, but this time I saw it go into diarrhoea.'

Whenever I feel pessimistic about the future of life on this earth,
I always return to this belief which I seem to have projected onto
the concept of evolutionary history. If we destroy this planet, then
I feel sure that this thing we call consciousness will *take off*, and
continue as an ever-developing entity, carrying the identity of the
next *creature species* in the eternal evolutionary reproductive system.

Consciousness is, after all, the great ultimate receptor of the whole potential of life as we know it here. I would love for there to be enough of me able to see that *moment* of emergence! I know I am projecting into the future – but who was it who said 'The future has already happened'?

I want to end with a few words which Dr Michael Fordham said recently in conversation. He said:

We may destroy ourselves, but we are part of the biological system which has always produced something superb and more complex. We may destroy our images of God, but they will crop up again somewhere else in human beings. *You can't destroy the thing they represent.*

10

DREAMS

The study of dreams has always been a central feature in therapeutic methods, both in diagnosis and treatment. The way a dream is used can vary with every patient and every therapist, although wide general guidelines have developed from the experience of successive exponents, as method and technique become organized in literature and practice.

So what is a dream?

I think of a dream as being a photograph; a snapshot of an area of the unconscious. The picture may be clear and straightforward, or more often like an aerial photograph which requires study under a lens to reveal detail and hidden features. Such study will lead to recognition and new perception of aspects, attitudes, functioning and knowledge. Revelation of this kind can provide guidance, wisdom, warning and stimulation, and lead to change and sometimes to the dynamic development of hitherto unused and unknown potential. To study a dream in this way is like taking a journey (preferably with a guide), into unfamiliar territory, aiming to expand and explain experience, or to reach a goal.

TYPES OF DREAMS

Like leaves on a tree, many dreams may look alike, but even in typical dreams there will be individual and subjective elements. Among countless examples, I can pick out just a few, including some frequent types and one or two rarer ones of deeper or momentous significance.

Nightmares

To deal with the nightmare, we need to bring the unconscious experience into conscious awareness – with great care; especially if it concerns a child. Children are often frightened and guilty if they have semi-conscious knowledge of things which they feel they *ought not to know*, or if their dreaming life is vibrating sources of vital racial experience or principles of myth and mystery.

DRAWING

One of the most fruitful methods of dream study is through drawing. Sometimes the whole dream can be illustrated, or perhaps certain details will develop in a series of pictures with astonishing revelations. Such a one was the drawing of a man's dream of being under a heavy stone slab – causing his whole body to be paralysed. There were many other features in this dream, and in discussing it all, nothing emerged until I suggested he should draw the stone slab by itself and carry it about in imagination to find a place to put it, in the drawings. It finished up lying in a graveyard, and he printed his father's name on the stone. I said:

'Why don't you set it up in the ground?'
He began to paint it set up in the earth, and to his astonishment the stone became a flowering tree. He said; 'I didn't think of this – the paint brush just got up and did it!'

He needed to find the right place to put his father's influence, so that it would grow and bear fruit, instead of carrying it as a heavy paralysing weight. He had not realized that the weight was his 'father', whom he regarded as 'such a good chap'. But the father's 'goodness' was also held by a heavy weight of strict religious authority.

PRISON DREAMS

I frequently hear dreams of people being in prison. These are often men's dreams. Here is an example from a young man who complained of being *stuck* in his life, but didn't know why.

'I was a prisoner in a room with three children, boys aged about three, five and fourteen. There were two warders, a man and a woman. The male warder was obviously in fear of the policewoman who seemed to be the real gaoler. The children were pale, hungry and frustrated, and kept appealing to me to free them. They seemed to be my children (I haven't any children in real life). I felt helpless and very doubtful for a long time, and then suddenly I got up and went over to the male warder and said; "There is no need to keep these children in prison. *You are a man!* Why don't you assert your authority and let them out? *I will help you.*" At this the male warder got up, took the keys from the policewoman – who did not resist – and opened the door, and we all went free.' End of dream.

'I felt a great weight had been lifted off me.'

Using the dream

Our discussion was short:

'Can you describe this weight?'
'It's been there all my life. I remember it first about the age of three, as though something held me back whenever I started to do anything I wanted to do. Either I got into trouble from adults, usually my mother, or I simply *couldn't do* it. It was much worse when I started school at five. The kids called me chicken and I could never play with them somehow. When I was fourteen it came over me like a great cloud, a real fog, and I really did get into prison then.'
'When you said to the warder, "You are a man, why don't you assert your authority?" who were you speaking to?'
'The male warder.'
'Who was he?'
'Someone quite unknown to me.'
'Why don't *you* let those children out?'
Here he became very agitated and said; 'Oh God! Does that mean *I* kept *myself* in prison? I suppose I must be the warders too!'

Once he had recognized these things as being in himself, we could begin work on his problem.

Someone recently quoted the following imaginary conversation:

A man appeals to God to rescue him from a pressing problem.
Man: 'Oh God! Are you there? Are you there?'
No reply.
With growing agitation: 'Oh God! Are you there, or am I speaking to myself?'
God: 'Oh man! Both are true!'

Symbolism

The study of dreams involves the study of symbols. These are the shorthand and the language of the Unconscious, with which it constructs its narratives and paints its pictures.

Almost always, a whole range of perception and information is telescoped and consolidated into a few symbolic pictures. Some techniques of interpretation suggest fixed symbols, whose meaning in any dream is always the same. I much prefer a pliable description in which a symbol can have different valid meanings in various dreams. Much can be missed, and its value lost if individual experience is suppressed by the introduction of a ready-made model. The model can get in the way of deeper knowledge, which may already be struggling against barriers to get out into awareness. This unique individual experience is often intuitive and instantaneous to the present moment. However, as long as this is understood, it is interesting and useful to look at some of the established and frequent dream symbols where a broad common meaning is relevant.

Dreams of Death

Death in a dream very rarely refers to physical death, but is a symbol of the metamorphosis principle. Like the phoenix, some part or attitude of a person may need its *death* in the fire, which alone can hatch out the continuing new life from its old form.

It is not so rare to experience oneself dying in a dream, and often this is the point of coming back to consciousness – waking up. To dream of someone else dying or being killed (even by oneself), will lead me to search more deeply into my psyche to discover what that person represents in me. We have Jung's example of his patient who dreamed his sister's two-year-old child had died. The man was glad because the *child* did not exist in reality, but represented an unfavourable two-year-old project of his sister's which he was glad to know had *died*.

Another very deep and impressive dream is described by a woman whose husband had died suddenly after thirty years of a well related marriage. She dreamed that she and her husband were coming together through a doorway out of a room they had been in, while the adjoining room had been completely gutted by fire, without affecting their room, or themselves. They came out of shadows into a bright light and she heard a voice say, 'You have an appointment with death.'

Study of this dream was very deep and vivid, and revealed her recognition of the *refining fire* of the Spirit which completed and initiated for her a new and continuing experience of relationship.

A Journey

Many dreams describe journeys, and significant points are contained in the method of travel, the purpose and goal of the journey, companions, obstacles, dangers, success or failure and so on. The *country* of the journey will be the dreamer's own psyche, and will relate to the way in which research into one's own unconscious is conducted or resisted; how hazards are dealt with, and what purposes are fulfilled or not. Means of travel are sometimes significant. For example, a train or a bus is a general carrier of the public, with its power, driver, conductor and guard all supplied and paid for. A car is more a family carrier and may be driven by oneself or a member of the family, for example. Finally, a pushbike is an individual carrier, proceeding on one's own independent power.

One contribution was from a woman who has had to take a lot of responsibility for others all her life.

Dreams of responsibility

'I was trying to guide a group of people through a difficult and hazardous mountain pass. It was in complete darkness and felt dangerous and almost impassable. I was responsible for them all and was struggling with a lot of thought and effort to see. Then I noticed that I had an old-fashioned bicycle lamp with me. But alas! The battery had run out. So I set off to find a battery.' End of dream.

Whatever this particular job signified in her own life, she is recognizing that the message of the dream is that she needs now to find her own individual *potential* (the battery) – to enable her to get the *group* (her own complex) through this particular hazard.

Dreams of animals

Animals are among the most frequent of all dream symbols, and represent various aspects of our instinctive functions and experience. Our physical body is animal with all its senses, needs, powers and energies of every kind. The way in which we accept and treat and are treated by animals in our dreams can tell us a lot about the way in which we experience these elements and aspects of ourselves. The energy of a horse is typical of our libidinal energy which can serve and work for us, run away with us, be wild or tame, and often will love us and be loved by us, and if well treated will bring us joy and fulfilment.

The snake has in general been given a phallic significance. This is often appropriate, but the snake or serpent is also a Christ symbol, and the medical snake of Aesculapius, too, is a symbol of healing.

Forgotten dreams

Some very short dreams can hold more significance than long, detailed descriptions, and I have found many dreams which people could not remember at all to have great and lasting usefulness. There are quite good ways of bringing a completely forgotten dream to consciousness, often through drawing.

A boy of sixteen said to me:

'I had a dream last night, but I can't remember it at all.'
I said: 'Draw it.'
'How the hell can I draw it if I can't remember it!'
'Here's some paper – draw it!'
Sulkily he drew two parallel lines across the paper.
'If the paper was bigger, would those lines continue?'

He added another sheet and continued with more and more elaboration of the lines. He added more sheets and more additions, and these drawings and our quite eager dialectic continued to develop for nine months, by which time his deep-seated problem had been tempted into consciousness by the developing drawings and our discussion of them. A very long dream indeed! The boy's problem had been a severe stammer which he lost completely after twelve months, as his extremely intuitive drawings explained it to him.

The Fall to Earth

In Richard Wilhelm's book, *The Secret of the Golden Flower* (1972), he describes the Oriental method by which the adept can spiritualize the semen instead of ejaculating it. The end of the description says,

'If this is not done, then the semen proceeds forwards, outwards, *falls to earth* and creates sons and daughters.' (This is *coitus reservatus*, not usually possible for occidental men.)

A talented musician and composer consulted me about a crippling phobia for heights which had worsened to a point where he could hardly go up onto an upper floor at home without panic. He told this dream:

'Shall Joan (his wife) – or shall she not – keep twenty white rabbits in the garden?'

That was the dream – just that question. Our conversation was brief.

'What associates to *twenty*?'

'We have been married twenty years.'

'What about the colour white?'

'Oh – easily seen, out in the light.'

'In the garden?'

'Oh yes – the same – all in the open – in full view – in public.'

'Rabbits?'

'Ugh! I don't like rabbits – they disgust me, they are such *breeders*!'

'Would Joan like rabbits in her garden?'

'Oh yes, she loves them.'

'Now tell me. When you are up on a height, what is the great fear?'

'Oh, it's the fall to earth.'

'What birth control do you use?'

'It's strange you should ask me that, because we have always used rather an unusual kind. I believe it's Eastern, where you don't ejaculate, but draw it back and absorb it.'

'Yes, it's called *coitus reservatus*, and if you *do* ejaculate it is called the *fall to earth* – which is what you are so afraid will happen.'

'So I suppose I have been afraid to bring the rabbity part of my marriage out into the light and talk about it?'

Dream People

The study of the people who visit us as we sleep provides a highly accessible route into the deeper area of the psyche where blockages are waiting to be removed, adventures asking to be undertaken, fears relieved, dangers averted, conflicts resolved and all the developmental work of the psyche carried forward. We have to remember that every person, every object, every event in a dream can represent characteristics, attitudes or styles of functioning in our own psyche. When a patient dreams of me – saying or doing something – I say,

'Why did *you* do (or say) that?' If the reply is, 'Oh, it wasn't me, it was *you* who did it', then I reply: 'But I wasn't there, you were lying in your bed asleep.' To see the dream person like this is especially useful if one is in reality experiencing problems or conflict with a real person. For example, someone has a habit of starting a quarrel with me, and in my dream is doing just that as usual. Deeper study, however, may reveal that, hiding deeper in my Unconscious, I have the same ability which, unknown to me, is being projected out on to this particular person, and so adding a quantity of my ability to quarrel to what is already there in the real person.

My animus

Many years ago I was enduring a problem of this kind in working with a male colleague, who seemed to cause continual conflict with me, however hard I tried to keep the peace. This was increasing to a point where I was beginning to feel persecuted by this man. Then I had a very vivid dream in which I got on a plane and went out to Zurich to see Jung. I explained at length, and Jung spoke only three words: 'It's your *animus*!'

I left, and then the journey began down into the contrasexual aspect of my personality to recognise how the *man in me* was causing, by projection, the increasing aggressiveness of the colleague.

These projections, however, are not always negative. You may discover through a dream that you really do possess yourself an ability or talent which you have admired or envied in someone else. When people tell me that I have given them a wise guidance in a dream I remind the dreamer that '*I*' in the dream was not me, but was '*your own inner analyst*'.

A colleague was discussing some problems she had, and for the whole hour she talked without pause. I sat silent in considerable admiration of her insight and wisdom about herself and the way she was working out solutions. At the end, she said to me, 'Oh! You are so wonderful, I wish I could have you to talk to me all the time.' I said 'Well, you can – take ME home with you.' 'Oh, if only I could', was her reply. I said 'You can – take ME off the "hook"!' Because what she was seeing as ME with its wisdom and competence was the projection of a part of herself, hung on a receptive 'hook' in my personality.

Warning Dreams

Warning as well as guidance is often found in dreams. One example of this was from a young therapy student whose energy and enthusiasm for the work was very rewarding to both of us. She dreamed that she was trapped deep down in an abyss among mountains where skiing was in progress. Full of anxiety she could see no way of getting out. Then she noticed an empty chair-lift hurtling overhead towards her on its way up the mountain. With a superhuman effort she jumped at it as it rushed over, and managed to cling onto the structure. Hanging perilously, she was rushed to the top, where it stopped with a jerk which shot her off in the snow. She wasn't hurt, but weak with fear and effort. She was quite agitated as she told me the dream, and when I said, 'the dream is a *warning*', she became even more anxious and started to explain how she had felt very apprehensive ever since the dream and indeed had felt it was a warning of danger. Then I said, '*The warning is to me* – not to rush you down into your unconscious and hurtle you back into conscious recognition too quickly.' 'Oh, that is a relief', she said, 'I was feeling we were going too fast, but I didn't feel it right for *me* to say so.'

Dreams Concerning Jung

As described in the Introduction, much of my learning and guidance in therapeutic work came from Jung's influence, most vividly in the many dreams of him which I was very fortunate to have.

Early in 1949 my interest in Jung's work was becoming especially stimulated, and his advice and challenge in these dreams was the greatest value to me in searching my own psyche.

My Sea

This dream occurred in 1949 when I was too eagerly plunging into the Unconscious and needed the reassurances of a stabilizing influence.

In the dream I found myself in the middle of the Atlantic Ocean: no land anywhere; no boat or companion. I was floating and felt I had to swim for my life. Then I realized that swimming was impossible, for my body was all in one piece, like a simple plastic doll with no limbs. The world I was within seemed to be a huge globe with its diameter the level ocean, the upper half the semi-circular sky, and the lower half the bowl of the sea. Jung seemed to be in the upper bowl, and I called to him for advice about my certain drowning. His vast voice answered from above me: 'What is it to drown?'

The echo of my answer reverberated from an unknown place below me in the ocean's depth: 'It is MY SEA.'

With that I let go into and within the water. I was absorbed into an infinite dimension of a bright wholeness of being, so that I seemed to become the water and the water equally became me. I woke gently and with a feeling of completeness.

If the water represented my unconscious – as it often does – then at that moment I felt very happy with my relation to it. At the same time I very much needed the courage to risk being 'drowned' by something I had not recognized was my own.

Three-mile swim (1957)

Again in the middle of the Atlantic Ocean where I had gone to rescue a five-year-old child. I had reached the boy and was supporting him, but felt the rescue swim was impossible. Again, I felt Jung's presence and appealed to him for advice. (It is interesting that in these situations of dilemma I did not at that time ask for actual help or protection, but for *advice*: That is, knowledge or confirmation of my own capacity.)

Jung asked: 'How far can you swim?'

I answered, 'Three miles.'

And Jung said with decision; 'Then we will make the shore three miles.'

(Once when young and with a strong swimmer companion and a following boat, I had swum three miles in the Devon sea. So this was the utmost I could do, and that was all I was asked to do.) With that I began to swim with the child. There was a transition and when next I was aware, the boy – now thirteen – and I were walking up the beach. End of dream.

I had to study what rescue had been demanded and carried out in that span of eight years. What part of myself had been neglected and left struggling in the Unconscious ocean up to that time? These were the first eight years of my analysis.

Search of a train

This dream is mentioned in the Introduction, and took place during the later stages of the conflict I was experiencing in developing my professional life: the conflict for dominance between the claims of intellectual theory and standardized forms of thought on the one hand; and on the other the opposite experience of unique, immediate, intuitive relation to *the individual soul*.

I was still having difficulty in accepting and using both in an equality of relationship, rather than in the former style of controversial opponents which had often seemed inevitable.

Animal Voices

Animals occur frequently in our dreams, and interpretations of their symbolism vary widely according to the individual dreamer and the climate and situation of the dream. I will include some dreams from my own experience in which the voices of the dream animals have emphasized again and again how I have needed to recognize and develop more fully that reconciliation and relationship between certain great opposite partners in the human psyche.

Animals very often speak to me in dreams, and have given me much valuable advice, and sometimes dramatic guidance and command. My Elephant appeared regularly during one period of intense learning and initiation. (See 'The Peacock's Lifecycle' Chapter 11.) Here are two more animal mentors from the Unconscious dream world.

The Cat (Head and Body)

The dream took place outside my childhood home, on a grass bank. My favourite black and white cat was lying stretched out on the ground and I was trying with a large axe to chop off its head. I knew I *had* to do this, but it was with a heavy confused inability that I kept on feebly chopping away at the cat's neck. My efforts were completely ineffective, and after some time, the cat raised her head and in an exasperated voice said: 'No, no! You'll never do it like that. Call your son!'

I called my sixteen-year-old son, who came out of the house whistling, and silently surveyed the scene. He took the axe from me without a word – raised it above his head and with one mighty blow, brought it down on the waiting neck like a guillotine. The severed head flew one way, the body another and all the internal organs gushed out. I shut my eyes in horror, and the boy put down the axe and returned to the house still whistling a cheerful tune. Then, out of that awesome silence I heard the contented voice of my lovely cat saying: 'There you are! I told you *he* would know how to do it!'

I opened my eyes, and there she was – my childhood companion – stretching out her limbs, purring and walking up towards me. End of dream.

The cat's message to me was that in my psyche, the relationship between 'head and body', (intellect and feeling), needed to be de-integrated and separated before they could be reunited in a more balanced partnership. My previous efforts to do this had been too weak and uncertain, still too biased and half-hearted. The task needed the strength and decisive courage of the 'son' – (part of the *animus*) – to accomplish it.

The Horse (Spirit and Earth)

In this dream, I was standing under the neck of an enormous horse whose back seemed to stretch up into the stratosphere. I knew I had to ride this huge creature. (Horses and I had a very special love relationship when I was a child, and I would often sit on a grazing horse free of harness in a field.) This, however, was terrifying and impossible to reach anywhere near its back. As usual, I found myself appealing to the mountain above me for advice. Like the profound echo of a great bell the answer descended to me in two commanding words: 'Know me!'

Tremblingly I looked up into the sky and stammered: 'I d-don't think I kn-ow you very well.'

At this the great creature bent down its monstrous head, bringing a cavernous open mouth right in front of my face, so that I was looking into a huge, toothed cave many times bigger than the whole of me. Out of this fearsome yawning chasm came a deep bass voice like a gentle roll of thunder: 'You will only get to know me by getting to know me.'

I shut my eyes in a surrender of joyful terror, and when I dared to open them the great horse had knelt down on the grass and I was sitting on its back with my arms round its neck, like a child on a favourite pony. End of dream.

The vital teaching of this horse dream was that I should recognize more deeply that the spiritual realm is not remote and unreachable, 'high up above the earth'. Nor is the instinctive animal realm isolated 'down below' in the physical world. The earth body contains the Spirit and all we call Divine. Thus the instinctive animal reaches to the limitless 'heights' and all that is there kneels on the green earth. So then they 'know each other'. In this symbolism we can see the gods – the primitive concept of the guidance and drive of instinctive patterns and functioning – and 'God', humanity's mental concept of the highest and most noble imagery of the Spirit.

If ever this union could be complete in the psyche of humanity, then there would be envisaged – the greatest Archetype of them all –

The primal final Unity
of the gods and God.

11

THE PEACOCK'S LIFECYCLE

WITH INTERPRETATION FROM C.G. JUNG

These eight pictures of my own were inspired by dreams which I had during the first three years of my analysis with one of C.G. Jung's colleagues. The analyst did not attempt to interpret the paintings but suggested that – as they were relevant to what Jung was writing at the time – they should be sent to Jung himself. This was agreed by Jung, and after studying them he wrote his commentary to me, an extract from which is printed below.

THE PEACOCK SERIES

The eight pictures, drawn mostly with coloured pencils, depict the lifecycle of the peacock, although they were not painted in the final sequence. For example, the two final ones – numbers 7 and 8 in the sequence (see p. 119) – were the second and third to be painted. As the production of the whole set spread over nearly two years, there is a special significance in this discrepancy. The drawings represented dreams and each time I had to wait for a dream to stand out from the habitual profusion in my sleeping. Then there would be some definite peacock reference which would initiate the drawing. Nearly all the pictures contain the brilliant feathers of the peacock's tail – *the bird of dawn*, and symbol of the phoenix. In his writing on alchemy, Jung likens the assembly of the colours in the peacock's tail to the alchemical process, so that it symbolizes the beginning and the end of the 'work'. Every one of the thousands of separate fronds in the feathers was done with a single pencil stroke, and each picture took many hours to complete. In one or two a little water-colour was added to obtain a special effect. I shall describe the drawings in the order in which they were produced, and assemble them in the correct sequence at the end.

'THE TUNNEL TO THE CENTRE' (PLATE 14)

The first picture sprang from a dream in which I found myself struggling to crawl through a narrow tube-like tunnel. It was transparent, and brilliantly coloured, and I recognized it as a quill of a feather in a peacock's tail. In the dream I seemed to be a little black bird with a broken wing. The bird, therefore, could not fly, but I felt sure that there was an urgent task in front of me – I had to crawl through every single frond of every feather to reach the centre. Here the body of the peacock stood bathed in the brightest golden-yellow light, and surrounded by the multicoloured spreading tail. The little black bird is just visible inside the centre of a feather on the lower right, from which point the long difficult journey begins.

THE TWO INTERPRETATIONS

Before presenting the rest of the series, I feel I should now tell you how there came to be two interpretations. In a letter to me Jung (1953) wrote the following:

> I have looked through your pictures with appreciation and admiration. The pictures belong to you, and you have painted them as a support to your own individuation process. As the Jongleur de Notre-Dame plays his tricks in honour of the Madonna, so you paint for the Self. In recognition of this fact, I am going to send the pictures back to you. They shouldn't be here, and nowhere else but with yourself, as they represent the approximation of the two worlds of spirit and body or of Ego and Self. The opposites seek each other so that the other side comes hither and the Here is swallowed by the There. In the last picture, both aspects approximately assume identity in producing a single circle. One could say a lot of things about such a central process. I have written quite a lot about it in my books, but they are not yet translated I am afraid.
>
> I thank you at all events for having shown me your pictures. I suppose it would be useful if you could contemplate these pictures until you feel that they are understood, as they contain a development not only of subjective importance, but also of a collective significance, viz. the substitution or development of the traditional and conventional Christian symbol to a symbol of totality. The latter is, as the church says, *implicite* in the Christian idea. From this point of view, you can see how much there is contained in your pictures.

Plate 14 The Tunnel to the Centre

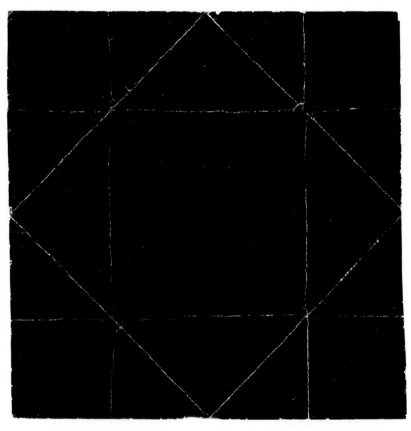

Plate 15 The Elephant and the Cathedral

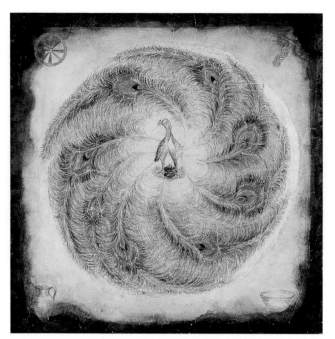

Plate 16 Parenthood

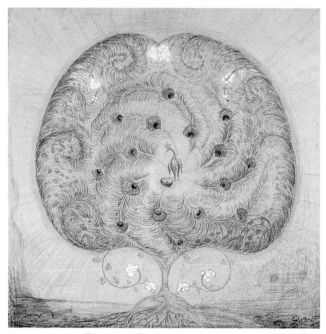

Plate 17 Adolescence

Plate 18 The Coitus

Plate 19 Death and Life

Plate 20 Nesting

Plate 21 Laying of the Egg

Plate 22 Final Sequence

The comments from Jung gave confirmation to one meaning of these dreams and pictures which had been intuitive to me after my third picture. It is the relating and integrating of Spirit and Body.

The Second Interpretation

The second vital meaning of this series, however, became fully conscious to me only after the fifth dream in the final series, and up to that time I had been satisfied with Jung's interpretation and my own intuition of the spiritual aspect. The associations now go back to my early childhood.

Washday in 1901

In 1901 I was two and a half, living in almost primitive conditions in a tiny hamlet in the very heart of the country, ten miles from a town, in an ancient 500-year-old farmhouse, with no facilities at all, like running water, gas or electricity. No shops, no telephone, no Post Office and so on.

Washday was a horrendous affair, every three weeks. Water had to be carried in buckets from nearby ponds, or tubs of rain water collected from roofs. It was heated in a huge brass cauldron hung on chains over a wood fire on the stone floor of the 'back kitchen'. Washing and wringing was done by hand. Soap was rubbed on and rinsing took place in one of the tubs set on upturned barrels. My mother employed a washerwoman from the hamlet to help. She came at 7.30am and stayed until 6.00pm. For this she was paid six pence, given three good meals, and sometimes extra food and clothes for her children. She had six children whose fathers seemed to have abandoned her. Not surprisingly she was a rather bitter, disillusioned woman; a fact which will have relevance later. She was a good washerwoman.

On this particular washday, when I was a little over two and a half, my mother and the washerwoman were hard at it, while I stood in the open doorway watching the chickens and ducks pecking about outside. Suddenly, the miller appeared in the doorway, with a one and a half hundredweight sack of corn on his shoulders. I knew him quite well, a friendly giant of a man. Now, what did I do? I did what I always did in those early days of Paradise. I flung my arms round his legs, and had my moment of ecstasy. You know the moment of ecstasy when you throw your arms round a man's legs? Especially if you are only two and a half! Well, there we stood – giant and child together. He said, 'Afternoon Mrs Cowley, I've braught yer karn, 'ull ye 'ave it shut?' [I've brought your corn, will you have it shot into the corn bin in the corner?] My mother dried her hands, and gently disengaged us. 'Come along now, we must let Mr Chapman put the corn in the bin for the chickens.'

I knew all about the corn and the chickens, so I did, and he did. Then he slung the empty sack on his shoulders and returned to the door where I was waiting. So what did I do? I did what I always did, for Paradise was not yet over – not quite. I threw my arms round his legs again, and the moment of ecstasy was prolonged, for he picked me up in his arms for a quick cuddle against the lovely smelly corn sack on his shoulder. Then he gently set me down and said, 'That's right little 'un, you know the way.'

You know the way! So this *was* the way. I had always thought so. Then he was gone with a wave and a whistle, and I remained in the erotic trance in the doorway ...

But – the bitter, disappointed washerwoman who had been so badly treated by men had been watching. She had seen and perceived it all. Waving a bar of soap at my mother, she said in a sour doom-laden voice: *'You'll have trouble with that child!'*

The trance shattered. Paradise was over. If the way was going to bring trouble to my mother, then perhaps it was forbidden and dangerous and impossible.

Like the Lady of Shallott:
'The mirror cracked from side to side.'
(A. Tennyson, 1923)

Thus was symbolized the long slow crawl through the thousands of narrow quills. A wing had been broken, so the little bird could not fly, the first vital energy was shackled. Early repression of natural erotic functioning clamped down on freedom and the journey was hard and difficult, and arrival at the golden goal at the centre was to be long delayed.

'THE ELEPHANT AND THE CATHEDRAL' (PLATE 15)

It was a long time before the next relevant dream inspired the second picture. In the dream, I had come into the Cathedral, (a frequent symbol in my dreams), to ask the Elephant for advice about this pressing problem of the baby bird. The Elephant also was a typical inhabitant of my dreaming life. He stood in front of the altar, and the first peacock drawing, (enlarged), was lying on the chancel floor. The Elephant – who always spoke in my dreams – answered me, but I could not translate the message. I cried out, 'But HOW?', and in reply he leaped upon the Peacock with a sound like thunder, and uttered one momentous word. This put the picture and the whole Cathedral into total darkness and I saw the four black corners of the picture fold over to form this black square. I woke, but could not recall that vital word.

The Black Square

In the evening I was still trying to recall that one crucial word which carried such important advice. The symbolism of the Elephant suggests the physical body and its wisdom – that emphatic largest body of all the earth's creatures.

I was at home talking to my husband in the kitchen during washing up – and after I had told him the dream, we were both striving to work out what the word could be. All I could recall was that it sounded like a word somewhere between the imposing 'Behold!' and the more superficial French 'Voyez! Voyez!'. As we puzzled over this, one of our sons, aged about thirteen, came out from the open door of an adjoining room where he had been reading, and said emphatically: 'I've heard what you were talking about – *I* know what that word is – it is *Discover* – you see – you must do it for yourself!'

Wisdom of the child indeed!

In the second interpretation it is clear how true was the essential emphasis on my own task of discovering how to complete the *journey* the body was undertaking.

So the sublime brilliance of the *bird of dawn* was covered in complete darkness as the four black corners of the painting folded over it. And my task was set – to discover a way through the long tunnel of the many thousand quills.

'PARENTHOOD' (PLATE 16)

This picture and the following one are numbers 7 and 8 in the final sequence, so that the real numbers 3, 4, 5 and 6 did not appear until these two last ones had been dreamed and painted. The significance of this is closely related to the second interpretation as we see how the long difficult climb to reach the ecstatic climax of experience has been by no means a straightforward process in my life. If the almost total repression of sexuality, 'the way' – symbolized by the washerwoman's prophecy – had not been prolonged throughout my childhood and adolescence, then perhaps the dream and drawing sequence would have been continuous.

From infancy, I had one overwhelming conscious aim, which filled the whole of my hopes and ambition. This was to have a baby. I was not concerned with the means to this goal, at least not consciously, and in my childhood such things were kept hidden from children as long as possible. So this third picture of parenthood and the birth of the baby had leaped across at intervening phases. Otherwise the third picture would have been 'The Coitus'.

This third painting has been my favourite, and depicts the parent peacocks embracing over the egg from which the new baby bird is emerging. The four figures in the corners represent the saying from Ecclesiastes:

> Or ever the silver cord be loosed,
> or the golden bowl be broken,
> or the pitcher broken at the fountain,
> or the wheel broken at the cistern;
> then shall the dust return to the earth as it was,
> and the Spirit shall return to God who gave it.
> (Old Testament, ch. 12, v. 6)

It was while painting this picture that I experienced the powerful intuition of the merging of Spirit and Body – as an abstract idea – and linked to the quotation. This was confirmed later by Jung.

'ADOLESCENCE' (PLATE 17)

This is the last (number 8) in the final sequence, and came very quickly after the *parent dream drawing*, as, naturally, the baby bird would grow through childhood. Here he is, growing his own tail, which is also a fruiting tree. The bodies of his parents have *returned to the earth*, as his independence develops, and they can be seen – still embracing – incorporated in the earth at the tree roots. Here their bodies contribute to the dark earth-substance surrounding the new adult bird. He would now be the first picture again as the cycle is repeated.

'THE COITUS' (NUMBER 3 IN FINAL SEQUENCE) (PLATE 18)

This drawing naturally would follow the black square in the final sequence. The coitus would be the next step for the young adult bird as he enters fatherhood. Strange isn't it, that there is, as yet, no female body there. She has to be drawn out of the darkness by the coital invitation, and this was the dream.

The Coitus dream took place again in the Cathedral. Once more the first picture covered in black was lying on the floor – this time in the nave. I was alone there and knew I was watching a momentous event. As I gazed at the blackness, (the whole Cathedral was also in darkness), a spot of yellow/red light appeared in the centre of the square. The light expanded and spread all over, lighting up the Cathedral as well, and when my eyes had grown accustomed to the brilliance, I beheld the vision of the Coitus, with the forming of the female body from the dark earth, as she yielded to her impregnation. The scene again includes a tree whose branches merge with the tail feathers. A tree is often symbolic of the Mother principle.

'DEATH AND LIFE' (NUMBER. 4 IN FINAL SEQUENCE) (PLATE 19)

Here is the female bird, already taking on the peacock colours as the pregnancy affects her whole body, proclaiming the creating of the new life within her. She is floating in a haze of upper atmospheric mist. Seen one way up, she looks as if dying, but turned up the other way she is rising into life. There was a very special reason for this. It was the only picture not inspired by a dream, but was painted with conscious intention.

Death of Juliet

I had been asked to visit Juliet – a girl of twenty-nine, who was dying of anorexia in a private nursing home. She was too near death for any psychotherapy, but wanted a 'Mother' to hold her through her passing. She had loved painting so I showed her the five paintings already done, and she asked me to paint one for her, 'to take with me on this unknown journey I am going on soon'. So I painted this one for her – 'Death and Life' – and she had it pinned on a screen by her bed. (The doctor told me later that she had said to him just before she died: 'I am going to sleep now and I shall go through that misty picture there into my new life.' She went to sleep at once and did not wake again.)

I intended this picture to show both death and life and, inspired by it, Juliet asked me to help her paint something herself. She couldn't sit up, but while I propped her up she managed to colour a black spot in the middle of a small page. At her request I turned it over and on the other side she expanded the back spot into a coloured spiral before she collapsed with fatigue.

I was seeing Juliet every other day – six times in all – and on my next visit she asked me to take the completed sequence of pictures to her mother from whom she had been slightly estranged. She asked especially that I should explain the death–rebirth theme to her mother. I promised her I would do this, but said I wanted to assemble the pictures in living order on one sheet. I was hesitating because I knew there should be a centre, and I couldn't decide what that should be. This dying girl struggled to raise herself, and with a gasping but emphatic breath she said, 'You put my black spot in the centre, and that will be enough.' She died a few hours later.

I carried out her wish when the assembled circle was complete, and found her mother was intensely moved and reconciled. The black spot in the centre followed her idea of an expanding spiral and spontaneously became the *silver cord* of the quotation.

'NESTING' AND 'LAYING OF THE EGG' (NUMBERS 5 AND 6 IN FINAL SEQUENCE) (PLATES 20 AND 21)

The two dreams of these two drawings were both almost daydreams – very near to consciousness – and both were dreamed at the same time. The first one shows the mother bird sitting on the nest laying the egg, with the father peacock feeding her. His tail is drooped as the care of her is now his priority. In the second, she has just laid the egg and is leaving the nest to prepare herself for the hatching routine. Apart from the black square, this picture is the only other one to have none of the peacock colour in it. It has always appealed to me as quiet and satisfied. The function is completed and the new life has started on its development. This was the last picture I painted, and I then assembled them in the final sequence on a single sheet (Plate 22). The four corners have the figures of the Ecclesiastes quotation, and the silver cord emerges from the black spot in the centre. The completed set was then shown to Juliet's mother, and after that sent to Jung.

The final sequence:

1. The adult peacock with spreading tail ('The Tunnel to the Centre').
2. The black square ('The Elephant and the Cathedral').
3. 'The Coitus'.
4. 'Death and Life'.
5. Pregnancy ('Nesting').
6. 'Laying of the Egg'.
7. Birth and 'Parenthood'.
8. 'Adolescence'.

FOUR JOURNEYS

Although I had been told of Juliet's death, nevertheless I visited the nursing home the next day at the time I would have seen her. The doctor took me into her room to return my peacock picture which was still pinned on her screen. He said, 'I wanted to give it back to you here', as he put it into my hands. Spontaneously I reversed the picture so that it showed the 'rising into life' aspect. Without a word the doctor took it again and pinned it in that position on her screen once more. We stood in silence for a while, and at last he said, 'I think that is what it meant to her.'

It is fitting that the book should approach its ending with Juliet's death and life experience together with the peacock's lifecycle, both leading into the short Epilogue which I have called 'The Therapeutic Journey'. The book as a whole is a record of journeys of research in which That Why Child took part, with so many companions and in so many situations, as my patients and I searched for the 'Why' and the purpose of our lives. We can focus on four of these journeys differing a great deal in the length of time the process lasted. Juliet's journeying with me lasted just twelve days from our first meeting. Nevertheless, her short experience of moving through life – through death to life again, as she felt it – represents that 'pulse in the eternal mind' whose contribution is no less than that of the ninety-seven-year-long journey of That Why Child, my fifty-year-long research into becoming a psychotherapist, or the twenty-year work of analysis. This began as a personal analysis, but developed into a profound research journey for both of us. For me, this became a deep and inspiring challenge to meet and enter into previously unacknowledged remote and awesome areas of the unconscious psyche. In all this, I have been vividly and gratefully aware of the mind of Jung. The contact with him began with my study of his writings, and became intensified and personal in the letters we exchanged after he had studied my pictures. More permanent and impressive has been the experience of many dreams I have had in which Jung would appear as himself, or as a voice or a pervading presence, giving me advice and support, or a strong challenge at points of crisis or dilemma in my outer or inner life. Dream conversations between us have continued, at times after his death, and even recently. In these ways I feel I have been privileged to count Jung as one of my companions on my therapeutic journey.

12

EPILOGUE
THE THERAPEUTIC JOURNEY

If Beethoven had arrived at a solution to the tragic problem of his deafness, he could have struck the chord of C major and ended his life work there. But what a loss to posterity it would have been if all that magnificent music of his later years had never been created out of his struggle to go on, in spite of a seemingly impossible problem.

This book has been about problems and therapy. Rather than arriving at solutions or the triumph of 'success', the endeavour has been to enable people to set out on a research journey into the resources of the human psyche, both individual and collective. The goal and the achievement lie in the releasing and using of those original potential energies with which a living creature is endowed.

Life's deep and serious problems are never fully solved. Complete satisfaction with reaching an apparent goal should be but the pause before renewing the research, for the purposeful meaning of a problem lies in its challenge and stimulation to continue working progressively around it.

When six-year-old Brian, terrified of the dark (Chapter 3, 'Children Thinking'), sat on my lap in total darkness, and he and I communed together, we must have set out on a journey into unconscious areas. There we could have touched some of those mysterious things which humanity has always feared. We did not arrive at a solution of such a vast collective problem. The subtle journey we took – literally hand in hand – inspired and strengthened the child to assemble his own resources, so that he could go forward, at a six-year-old level, through the immediate problematic situation – which he himself had created. He then took command of himself, of me and of the event. This was his 'success', and the kind of therapy which he could best make use of.

Most therapy is a response to the urgent needs of people to recover from childhood, and to rescue the potential 'child' whose original native energies have been stultified and imprisoned by environmental conditions, or pressures from authorities and culture. This child rescue is the basic principle of all our therapy, often symbolized in dreams by a continuous journey or effort to save a child from danger or imprisonment: for example, the three-mile swim with a boy, representing eight years of analytic therapy (Chapter 10, 'Dreams'). The process is the same, whether it is an actual child, or the 'child' in an adult which needs to be released.

A woman seeking analytical therapy was asked at her first interview, 'Why do you want analysis?' She told me afterwards that she had not had a ready answer, but to her extreme astonishment she heard a child's voice say, 'I must be what I am.'

This book began with the experience of a child, so let the words of five-year-old Robin complete it (Chapter 3, 'Children Thinking'). When asked what he wanted to *be* when older, he said:

'I don't want to be *anything* – I want to be ME!'

REFERENCES

Baynes H.G. (1949) 'Mythology of the Soul'. Introduction. Published by Methuen & Co. Ltd.

Bettelheim B. (1950) 'Love is not Enough'. Published by Collier Macmillan, London.

Donne J. (1936) 'Nocturnal upon St. Lucie's Day'. Published by Nonesuch Press, London.

Dryden J. (1935) 'Alexander's Feast' Gems of National Poetry. Published by Oxford University Press.

Ecclesiastes Old Testament. Chapter 12. Verse 6.

Fordham M. Introduction to this Edition.

Fordham M. (1992) Reported conversation with Carol Jeffrey.

Freud S. (1985) *The Complete Letters of Sigmund Freud and Wilhelm Fliess, 1887–1904*. Published by Harvard University Press.

Howe G. (1939) The Open Way Charitable Trust 'A Study of Acceptance'. Published by John M. Watkins, London.

Jeffrey C. 'Conjunctio' Author's Poem unpublished.

Jung C.G. (1953) 'C.G. Jung Letters Volume 2'. Published by Routledge & Kegan Paul. Edited by G. Adler.

Jung C.G. (1959) 'Archetypes and the Collective Unconscious'. Published by Routledge & Kegan Paul.

Massey G. 'The Bridegroom of Beauty'. 1828–1907 Poems – edited by Stevenson.

Sheldrake R. (1981) *A New Science of Life*. Published by Blond and Briggs, London.

Tennyson A. (1923) 'Lady of Shallott' Poems. Published by Oxford University Press.

Watson G. (1949) (unpublished) Guild of Pastoral Psychology Lecture, London.

Watts A. (1950s) Private Communication.

Wilhelm R. (1972) 'The Secret of the Golden Flower'. Published by Routledge & Kegan Paul.

INDEX